Disruptive
Artificial Intelligence (AI)
And
Driverless Self-Driving Cars

Practical Advances in Artificial Intelligence (AI) and Machine Learning

Dr. Lance B. Eliot, MBA, PhD

ISBN: 0692131973
ISBN-13: 978-0692131978

DEDICATION

To my incredible daughter, Lauren and my incredible son, Michael.

Forest fortuna adiuvat (from the Latin; good fortune favors the brave).

CONTENTS

Lance B. Eliot

ACKNOWLEDGMENTS

I have been the beneficiary of advice and counsel by many friends, colleagues, family, investors, and many others. I want to thank everyone that has aided me throughout my career. I write from the heart and the head, having experienced first-hand what it means to have others around you that support you during the good times and the tough times.

To Warren Bennis, one of my doctoral advisors and ultimately a colleague, I offer my deepest thanks and appreciation, especially for his calm and insightful wisdom and support.

To Mark Stevens and his generous efforts toward funding and supporting the USC Stevens Center for Innovation.

To Lloyd Greif and the USC Lloyd Greif Center for Entrepreneurial Studies for their ongoing encouragement of founders and entrepreneurs.

To Peter Drucker, William Wang, Aaron Levie, Peter Kim, Jon Kraft, Cindy Crawford, Jenny Ming, Steve Milligan, Chis Underwood, Frank Gehry, Buzz Aldrin, Steve Forbes, Bill Thompson, Dave Dillon, Alan Fuerstman, Larry Ellison, Jim Sinegal, John Sperling, Mark Stevenson, Anand Nallathambi, Thomas Barrack, Jr., and many other innovators and leaders that I have met and gained mightily from doing so.

Thanks to Ed Trainor, Kevin Anderson, James Hickey, Wendell Jones, Ken Harris, DuWayne Peterson, Mike Brown, Jim Thornton, Abhi Beniwal, Al Biland, John Nomura, Eliot Weinman, John Desmond, and many others for their unwavering support during my career.

And most of all thanks as always to Lauren and Michael, for their ongoing support and for having seen me writing and heard much of this material during the many months involved in writing it. To their patience and willingness to listen.

Lance B. Eliot

INTRODUCTION

This is a book that provides the newest innovations and the latest Artificial Intelligence (AI) advances about the emerging nature of AI-based autonomous self-driving driverless cars. Via recent advances in Artificial Intelligence (AI) and Machine Learning (ML), we are nearing the day when vehicles can control themselves and will not require and nor rely upon human intervention to perform their driving tasks (or, that <u>allow</u> for human intervention, but only *require* human intervention in very limited ways).

Similar to my other related books, which I describe in a moment and list the chapters in the Appendix A of this book, I am particularly focused on those advances that pertain to self-driving cars. The phrase "autonomous vehicles" is often used to refer to any kind of vehicle, whether it is ground-based or in the air or sea, and whether it is a cargo hauling trailer truck or a conventional passenger car. Though the aspects described in this book are certainly applicable to all kinds of autonomous vehicles, I am focused more so here on cars.

Indeed, I am especially known for my role in aiding the advancement of self-driving cars, serving currently as the Executive Director of the Cybernetic Self-Driving Cars Institute.. In addition to writing software, designing and developing systems and software for self-driving cars, I also speak and write quite a bit about the topic. This book is a collection of some of my more advanced essays. For those of you that might have seen my essays posted elsewhere, I have updated them and integrated them into this book as one handy cohesive package.

You might be interested in companion books that I have written that provide additional key innovations and fundamentals about self-driving cars. Those books are entitled **"Introduction to Driverless Self-Driving Cars," "Advances in AI and Autonomous Vehicles: Cybernetic Self-Driving Cars," "Self-Driving Cars: "The Mother of All AI Projects," "Innovation and Thought Leadership on Self-Driving Driverless Cars," "New Advances in AI Autonomous Driverless Self-Driving Cars,"** and **"Autonomous Vehicle Driverless Self-Driving Cars and**

Artificial Intelligence" and **"Transformative Artificial Intelligence Driverless Self-Driving Cars"** (they are all available via Amazon). See Appendix A of this herein book to see a listing of the chapters covered in those three books.

For the introduction here to this book, I am going to borrow my introduction from those companion books, since it does a good job of laying out the landscape of self-driving cars and my overall viewpoints on the topic. The remainder of the book is all new material that does not appear in the companion books.

INTRODUCTION TO SELF-DRIVING CARS

This is a book about self-driving cars. Someday in the future, we'll all have self-driving cars and this book will perhaps seem antiquated, but right now, we are at the forefront of the self-driving car wave. Daily news bombards us with flashes of new announcements by one car maker or another and leaves the impression that within the next few weeks or maybe months that the self-driving car will be here. A casual non-technical reader would assume from these news flashes that in fact we must be on the cusp of a true self-driving car.

Here's a real news flash: We are still quite a distance from having a true self-driving car. It is years to go before we get there.

Why is that? Because a true self-driving car is akin to a moonshot. In the same manner that getting us to the moon was an incredible feat, likewise can it be said for achieving a true self-driving car. Anybody that suggests or even brashly states that the true self-driving car is nearly here should be viewed with great skepticism. Indeed, you'll see that I often tend to use the word "hogwash" or "crock" when I assess much of the decidedly *fake news* about self-driving cars. Those of us on the inside know that what is often reported to the outside is malarkey. Few of the insiders are willing to say so. I have no such hesitation.

Indeed, I've been writing a popular blog post about self-driving cars and hitting hard on those that try to wave their hands and pretend that we are on the imminent verge of true self-driving cars. For many years, I've been known as the AI Insider. Besides writing about AI, I also develop AI software. I do what I describe. It also gives me insights into what others that are doing AI are really doing versus what it is said they are doing.

Many faithful readers had asked me to pull together my insightful short essays and put them into another book, which you are now holding in your hands.

For those of you that have been reading my essays over the years, this collection not only puts them together into one handy package, I also updated the essays and added new material. For those of you that are new to the topic of self-driving cars and AI, I hope you find these essays approachable and informative. I also tend to have a writing style with a bit of a voice, and so you'll see that I am times have a wry sense of humor and also like to poke at conformity.

As a former professor and founder of an AI research lab, I for many years wrote in the formal language of academic writing. I published in referred journals and served as an editor for several AI journals. This writing here is not of the nature, and I have adopted a different and more informal style for these essays. That being said, I also do mention from time-to-time more rigorous material on AI and encourage you all to dig into those deeper and more formal materials if so interested.

I am also an AI practitioner. This means that I write AI software for a living. Currently, I head-up the Cybernetics Self-Driving Car Institute, where we are developing AI software for self-driving cars. I am excited to also report that my son, also a software engineer, heads-up our Cybernetics Self-Driving Car Lab. What I have helped to start, and for which he is an integral part, ultimately he will carry long into the future after I have retired. My daughter, a marketing whiz, also is integral to our efforts as head of our Marketing group. She too will carry forward the legacy now being formulated.

For those of you that are reading this book and have a penchant for writing code, you might consider taking a look at the open source code available for self-driving cars. This is a handy place to start learning how to develop AI for self-driving cars. There are also many new educational courses spring forth.

There is a growing body of those wanting to learn about and develop self-driving cars, and a growing body of colleges, labs, and other avenues by which you can learn about self-driving cars.

This book will provide a foundation of aspects that I think will get you ready for those kinds of more advanced training opportunities. If you've already taken those classes, you'll likely find these essays especially interesting as they offer a perspective that I am betting few other instructors or faculty offered to you. These are challenging essays that ask you to think beyond the conventional about self-driving cars.

THE MOTHER OF ALL AI PROJECTS

In June 2017, Apple CEO Tim Cook came out and finally admitted that Apple has been working on a self-driving car. As you'll see in my essays, Apple was enmeshed in secrecy about their self-driving car efforts. We have only been able to read the tea leaves and guess at what Apple has been up to.

The notion of an iCar has been floating for quite a while, and self-driving engineers and researchers have been signing tight-lipped Non-Disclosure Agreements (NDA's) to work on projects at Apple that were as shrouded in mystery as any military invasion plans might be.

Tim Cook said something that many others in the Artificial Intelligence (AI) field have been saying, namely, the creation of a self-driving car has got to be the mother of all AI projects. In other words, it is in fact a tremendous moonshot for AI. If a self-driving car can be crafted and the AI works as we hope, it means that we have made incredible strides with AI and that therefore it opens many other worlds of potential breakthrough accomplishments that AI can solve.

Is this hyperbole? Am I just trying to make AI seem like a miracle worker and so provide self-aggrandizing statements for those of us writing the AI software for self-driving cars? No, it is not hyperbole. Developing a true self-driving car is really, really, really hard to do. Let me take a moment to explain why. As a side note, I realize that the Apple CEO is known for at times uttering hyperbole, and he had previously said for example that the year 2012 was "the mother of all years," and he had said that the release of iOS 10 was "the mother of all releases" – all of which does suggest he likes to use the handy "mother of" expression. But, I assure you, in terms of true self-driving cars, he has hit the nail on the head. For sure.

When you think about a moonshot and how we got to the moon, there are some identifiable characteristics and those same aspects can be applied to creating a true self-driving car. You'll notice that I keep putting the word "true" in front of the self-driving car expression. I do so because as per my essay about the various levels of self-driving cars (see Chapter 3), there are some self-driving cars that are only somewhat of a self-driving car. The somewhat versions are ones that require a human driver to be ready to intervene. In my view, that's not a true self-driving car. A true self-driving car is one that requires no human driver intervention at all. It is a car that can entirely undertake via automation the driving task without any human driver needed. This is the essence of what is known as a Level 5 self-driving car. We are currently at the Level 2 and Level 3 mark, and not yet at Level 5.

Getting to the moon involved aspects such as having big stretch goals, incremental progress, experimentation, innovation, and so on. Let's review how this applied to the moonshot of the bygone era, and how it applies to the self-driving car moonshot of today.

Big Stretch Goal

Trying to take a human and deliver the human to the moon, and bring them back, safely, was an extremely large stretch goal at the time. No one knew whether it could be done. The technology wasn't available yet. The cost was huge. The determination would need to be fierce. Etc. To reach a Level 5 self-driving car is going to be the same. It is a big stretch goal. We can readily get to the Level 3, and we are able to see the Level 4 just up ahead, but a Level 5 is still an unknown as to if it is doable. It should eventually be doable and in the same way that we thought we'd eventually get to the moon, but when it will occur is a different story.

Incremental Progress

Getting to the moon did not happen overnight in one fell swoop. It took years and years of incremental progress to get there. Likewise for self-driving cars. Google has famously been striving to get to the Level 5, and pretty much been willing to forgo dealing with the intervening levels, but most of the other self-driving car makers are doing the incremental route. Let's get a good Level 2 and a somewhat Level 3 going. Then, let's improve the Level 3 and get a somewhat Level 4 going. Then, let's improve the Level 4 and finally arrive at a Level 5. This seems to be the prevalent way that we are going to achieve the true self-driving car.

Experimentation

You likely know that there were various experiments involved in perfecting the approach and technology to get to the moon. As per making incremental progress, we first tried to see if we could get a rocket to go into space and safety return, then put a monkey in there, then with a human, then we went all the way to the moon but didn't land, and finally we arrived at the mission that actually landed on the moon. Self-driving cars are the same way. We are doing simulations of self-driving cars. We do testing of self-driving cars on private land under controlled situations. We do testing of self-driving cars on public roadways, often having to meet regulatory requirements including for example having an engineer or equivalent in the car to take over the controls if needed. And so on. Experiments big and small are needed to figure out what works and what doesn't.

Innovation

There are already some advances in AI that are allowing us to progress toward self-driving cars. We are going to need even more advances. Innovation in all aspects of technology are going to be required to achieve a true self-driving car. By no means do we already have everything in-hand that we need to get there. Expect new inventions and new approaches, new algorithms, etc.

Setbacks

Most of the pundits are avoiding talking about potential setbacks in the progress toward self-driving cars. Getting to the moon involved many setbacks, some of which you never have heard of and were buried at the time so as to not dampen enthusiasm and funding for getting to the moon. A recurring theme in many of my included essays is that there are going to be setbacks as we try to arrive at a true self-driving car. Take a deep breath and be ready. I just hope the setbacks don't completely stop progress. I am sure that it will cause progress to alter in a manner that we've not yet seen in the self-driving car field. I liken the self-driving car of today to the excitement everyone had for Uber when it first got going. Today, we have a different view of Uber and with each passing day there are more regulations to the ride sharing business and more concerns raised. The darling child only stays a darling until finally that child acts up. It will happen the same with self-driving cars.

SELF-DRIVING CARS CHALLENGES

But what exactly makes things so hard to have a true self-driving car, you might be asking. You have seen cruise control for years and years. You've lately seen cars that can do parallel parking. You've seen YouTube videos of Tesla drivers that put their hands out the window as their car zooms along the highway, and seen to therefore be in a self-driving car. Aren't we just needing to put a few more sensors onto a car and then we'll have in-hand a true self-driving car? Nope.

Consider for a moment the nature of the driving task. We don't just let anyone at any age drive a car. Worldwide, most countries won't license a driver until the age of 18, though many do allow a learner's permit at the age of 15 or 16. Some suggest that a younger age would be physically too small to reach the controls of the car. Though this might be the case, we could easily adjust the controls to allow for younger aged and thus smaller stature. It's not their physical size that matters. It's their cognitive development that matters.

To drive a car, you need to be able to reason about the car, what the car can and cannot do. You need to know how to operate the car. You need to know about how other cars on the road drive. You need to know what is allowed in driving such as speed limits and driving within marked lanes. You need to be able to react to situations and be able to avoid getting into accidents. You need to ascertain when to hit your brakes, when to steer clear of a pedestrian, and how to keep from ramming that motorcyclist that just cut you off.

Many of us had taken courses on driving. We studied about driving and took driver training. We had to take a test and pass it to be able to drive. The point being that though most adults take the driving task for granted, and we often "mindlessly" drive our cars, there is a significant amount of cognitive effort that goes into driving a car. After a while, it becomes second nature. You don't especially think about how you drive, you just do it. But, if you watch a novice driver, say a teenager learning to drive, you suddenly realize that there is a lot more complexity to it than we seem to realize.

Furthermore, driving is a very serious task. I recall when my daughter and son first learned to drive. They are both very conscientious people. They wanted to make sure that whatever they did, they did well, and that they did not harm anyone. Every day, when you get into a car, it is probably around 4,000 pounds of hefty metal and plastics (about two tons), and it is a lethal weapon. Think about it. You drive down the street in an object that weighs two tons and with the engine it can accelerate and ram into anything you want to hit. The damage a car can inflict is very scary. Both my children were surprised that they were being given the right to maneuver this monster of a beast that could cause tremendous harm entirely by merely letting go of the steering wheel for a moment or taking your eyes off the road.

In fact, in the United States alone there are about 30,000 deaths per year by auto accidents, which is around 100 per day. Given that there are about 263 million cars in the United States, I am actually more amazed that the number of fatalities is not a lot higher. During my morning commute, I look at all the thousands of cars on the freeway around me, and I think that if all of them decided to go zombie and drive in a crazy maniac way, there would be many people dead. Somehow, incredibly, each day, most people drive relatively safely. To me, that's a miracle right there. Getting millions and millions of people to be safe and sane when behind the wheel of a two ton mobile object, it's a feat that we as a society should admire with pride.

So, hopefully you are in agreement that the driving task requires a great deal of cognition. You don't' need to be especially smart to drive a car, and we've done quite a bit to make car driving viable for even the average dolt. There isn't an IQ test that you need to take to drive a car. If you can read and write, and pass a test, you pretty much can legally drive a car. There are of course some that drive a car and are not legally permitted to do so, plus there are private areas such as farms where drivers are young, but for public roadways in the United States, you can be generally of average intelligence (or less) and be able to legally drive.

This though makes it seem like the cognitive effort must not be much. If the cognitive effort was truly hard, wouldn't we only have Einstein's that could drive a car? We have made sure to keep the driving task as simple as we can, by making the controls easy and relatively standardized, and by having roads that are relatively standardized, and so on. It is as though Disneyland has put their Autopia into the real-world, by us all as a society agreeing that roads will be a certain way, and we'll all abide by the various rules of driving.

A modest cognitive task by a human is still something that stymies AI. You certainly know that AI has been able to beat chess players and be good at other kinds of games. This type of narrow cognition is not what car driving is about. Car driving is much wider. It requires knowledge about the world, which a chess playing AI system does not need to know. The cognitive aspects of driving are on the one hand seemingly simple, but at the same time require layer upon layer of knowledge about cars, people, roads, rules, and a myriad of other "common sense" aspects. We don't have any AI systems today that have that same kind of breadth and depth of awareness and knowledge.

As revealed in my essays, the self-driving car of today is using trickery to do particular tasks. It is all very narrow in operation. Plus, it currently assumes that a human driver is ready to intervene. It is like a child that we have taught to stack blocks, but we are needed to be right there in case the child stacks them too high and they begin to fall over. AI of today is brittle, it is narrow, and it does not approach the cognitive abilities of humans. This is why the true self-driving car is somewhere out in the future.

Another aspect to the driving task is that it is not solely a mind exercise. You do need to use your senses to drive. You use your eyes a vision sensors to see the road ahead. You vision capability is like a streaming video, which your brain needs to continually analyze as you drive. Where is the road? Is there a pedestrian in the way? Is there another car ahead of you? Your senses are relying a flood of info to your brain. Self-driving cars are trying to do the same, by using cameras, radar, ultrasound, and lasers. This is an attempt at mimicking how humans have senses and sensory apparatus.

Thus, the driving task is mental and physical. You use your senses, you use your arms and legs to manipulate the controls of the car, and you use your brain to assess the sensory info and direct your limbs to act upon the controls of the car. This all happens instantly. If you've ever perhaps gotten something in your eye and only had one eye available to drive with, you suddenly realize how dependent upon vision you are. If you have a broken foot with a cast, you suddenly realize how hard it is to control the brake pedal and the accelerator. If you've taken medication and your brain is maybe sluggish, you suddenly realize how much mental strain is required to drive a car.

An AI system that plays chess only needs to be focused on playing chess. The physical aspects aren't important because usually a human moves the chess pieces or the chessboard is shown on an electronic display. Using AI for a more life-and-death task such as analyzing MRI images of patients, this again does not require physical capabilities and instead is done by examining images of bits.

Driving a car is a true life-and-death task. It is a use of AI that can easily and at any moment produce death. For those colleagues of mine that are developing this AI, as am I, we need to keep in mind the somber aspects of this. We are producing software that will have in its virtual hands the lives of the occupants of the car, and the lives of those in other nearby cars, and the lives of nearby pedestrians, etc. Chess is not usually a life-or-death matter.

Driving is all around us. Cars are everywhere. Most of today's AI applications involve only a small number of people. Or, they are behind the scenes and we as humans have other recourse if the AI messes up. AI that is driving a car at 80 miles per hour on a highway had better not mess up. The consequences are grave. Multiply this by the number of cars, if we could put magically self-driving into every car in the USA, we'd have AI running in the 263 million cars. That's a lot of AI spread around. This is AI on a massive scale that we are not doing today and that offers both promise and potential peril.

There are some that want AI for self-driving cars because they envision a world without any car accidents. They envision a world in which there is no car congestion and all cars cooperate with each other. These are wonderful utopian visions.

They are also very misleading. The adoption of self-driving cars is going to be incremental and not overnight. We cannot economically just junk all existing cars. Nor are we going to be able to affordably retrofit existing cars. It is more likely that self-driving cars will be built into new cars and that over many years of gradual replacement of existing cars that we'll see the mix of self-driving cars become substantial in the real-world.

In these essays, I have tried to offer technological insights without being overly technical in my description, and also blended the business, societal, and economic aspects too. Technologists need to consider the non-technological impacts of what they do. Non-technologists should be aware of what is being developed.

We all need to work together to collectively be prepared for the enormous disruption and transformative aspects of true self-driving cars. We all need to be involved in this mother of all AI projects.

WHAT THIS BOOK PROVIDES

What does this book provide to you? It introduces many of the key elements about self-driving cars and does so with an AI based perspective. I weave together technical and non-technical aspects, readily going from being concerned about the cognitive capabilities of the driving task and how the technology is embodying this into self-driving cars, and in the next breath I discuss the societal and economic aspects.

They are all intertwined because that's the way reality is. You cannot separate out the technology per se, and instead must consider it within the milieu of what is being invented and innovated, and do so with a mindset towards the contemporary mores and culture that shape what we are doing and what we hope to do.

WHY THIS BOOK

I wrote this book to try and bring to the public view many aspects about self-driving cars that nobody seems to be discussing.

For business leaders that are either involved in making self-driving cars or that are going to leverage self-driving cars, I hope that this book will enlighten you as to the risks involved and ways in which you should be strategizing about how to deal with those risks.

For entrepreneurs, startups and other businesses that want to enter into the self-driving car market that is emerging, I hope this book sparks your interest in doing so, and provides some sense of what might be prudent to pursue.

For researchers that study self-driving cars, I hope this book spurs your interest in the risks and safety issues of self-driving cars, and also nudges you toward conducting research on those aspects.

For students in computer science or related disciplines, I hope this book will provide you with interesting and new ideas and material, for which you might conduct research or provide some career direction insights for you.

For AI companies and high-tech companies pursuing self-driving cars, this book will hopefully broaden your view beyond just the mere coding and development needed to make self-driving cars.

For all readers, I hope that you will find the material in this book to be stimulating. Some of it will be repetitive of things you already know. But I am pretty sure that you'll also find various eureka moments whereby you'll discover a new technique or approach that you had not earlier thought of. I am also betting that there will be material that forces you to rethink some of your current practices.

I am not saying you will suddenly have an epiphany and change what you are doing. I do think though that you will reconsider or perhaps revisit what you are doing.

For anyone choosing to use this book for teaching purposes, please take a look at my suggestions for doing so, as described in the Appendix. I have found the material handy in courses that I have taught, and likewise other faculty have told me that they have found the material handy, in some cases as extended readings and in other instances as a core part of their course (depending on the nature of the class).

In my writing for this book, I have tried carefully to blend both the practitioner and the academic styles of writing. It is not as dense as is typical academic journal writing, but at the same time offers depth by going into the nuances and trade-offs of various practices.

The word "deep" is in vogue today, meaning getting deeply into a subject or topic, and so is the word "unpack" which means to tease out the underlying aspects of a subject or topic. I have sought to offer material that addresses an issue or topic by going relatively deeply into it and make sure that it is well unpacked.

Finally, in any book about AI, it is difficult to use our everyday words without having some of them be misinterpreted. Specifically, it is easy to anthropomorphize AI. When I say that an AI system "knows" something, I do not want you to construe that the AI system has sentience and "knows" in the same way that humans do. They aren't that way, as yet. I have tried to use quotes around such words from time-to-time to emphasize that the words I am using should not be misinterpreted to ascribe true human intelligence to the AI systems that we know of today. If I used quotes around all such words, the book would be very difficult to read, and so I am doing so judiciously. Please keep that in mind as you read the material, thanks.

COMPANION BOOKS

If you find this material of interest, you might want to also see my other books on self-driving cars, entitled:

1. **"Introduction to Driverless Self-Driving Cars"** by Dr. Lance Eliot

2. **"Innovation and Thought Leadership on Self-Driving Driverless Cars"** by Dr. Lance Eliot

3. **"Advances in AI and Autonomous Vehicles: Cybernetic Self-Driving Cars"** by Dr. Lance Eliot

4. *"Self-Driving Cars: The Mother of All AI Projects"* by Dr. Lance Eliot

5. **"New Advances in AI Autonomous Driverless Self-Driving Cars"** by Dr. Lance Eliot

6. **"Autonomous Vehicle Driverless Self-Driving Cars and Artificial Intelligence"** by Dr. Lance Eliot and Michael B. Eliot

7. **"Transformative Artificial Intelligence Driverless Self-Driving Cars"** by Dr. Lance Eliot

All of the above books are available on Amazon and at other major global booksellers.

CHAPTER 1

ELIOT FRAMEWORK FOR AI SELF-DRIVING CARS

CHAPTER 1

ELIOT FRAMEWORK FOR AI SELF-DRIVING CARS

This chapter is a core foundational aspect for understanding AI self-driving cars and I have used this same chapter in several of my other books to introduce the reader to essential elements of this field. Once you've read this chapter, you'll be prepared to read the rest of the material since the foundational essence of the components of autonomous AI driverless self-driving cars will have been established for you.

———————

When I give presentations about self-driving cars and teach classes on the topic, I have found it helpful to provide a framework around which the various key elements of self-driving cars can be understood and organized (see diagram at the end of this chapter). The framework needs to be simple enough to convey the overarching elements, but at the same time not so simple that it belies the true complexity of self-driving cars. As such, I am going to describe the framework here and try to offer in a thousand words (or more!) what the framework diagram itself intends to portray.

The core elements on the diagram are numbered for ease of reference. The numbering does not suggest any kind of prioritization of the elements. Each element is crucial. Each element has a purpose, and otherwise would not be included in the framework. For some self-driving cars, a particular element might be more important or somehow distinguished in comparison to other self-driving cars.

You could even use the framework to rate a particular self-driving car, doing so by gauging how well it performs in each of the elements of the framework. I will describe each of the elements, one at a time. After doing so, I'll discuss aspects that illustrate how the elements interact and perform during the overall effort of a self-driving car.

At the Cybernetic Self-Driving Car Institute, we use the framework to keep track of what we are working on, and how we are developing software that fills in what is needed to achieve Level 5 self-driving cars.

D-01: Sensor Capture

Let's start with the one element that often gets the most attention in the press about self-driving cars, namely, the sensory devices for a self-driving car.

On the framework, the box labeled as D-01 indicates "Sensor Capture" and refers to the processes of the self-driving car that involve collecting data from the myriad of sensors that are used for a self-driving car. The types of devices typically involved are listed, such as the use of mono cameras, stereo cameras, LIDAR devices, radar systems, ultrasonic devices, GPS, IMU, and so on.

These devices are tasked with obtaining data about the status of the self-driving car and the world around it. Some of the devices are continually providing updates, while others of the devices await an indication by the self-driving car that the device is supposed to collect data. The data might be first transformed in some fashion by the device itself, or it might instead be fed directly into the sensor capture as raw data. At that point, it might be up to the sensor capture processes to do transformations on the data. This all varies depending upon the nature of the devices being used and how the devices were designed and developed.

D-02: Sensor Fusion

Imagine that your eyeballs receive visual images, your nose receives odors, your ears receive sounds, and in essence each of your distinct sensory devices is getting some form of input. The input befits the nature of the device. Likewise, for a self-driving car, the cameras provide visual images, the radar returns radar reflections, and so on.

Each device provides the data as befits what the device does.

At some point, using the analogy to humans, you need to merge together what your eyes see, what your nose smells, what your ears hear, and piece it all together into a larger sense of what the world is all about and what is happening around you. Sensor fusion is the action of taking the singular aspects from each of the devices and putting them together into a larger puzzle.

Sensor fusion is a tough task. There are some devices that might not be working at the time of the sensor capture. Or, there might some devices that are unable to report well what they have detected. Again, using a human analogy, suppose you are in a dark room and so your eyes cannot see much. At that point, you might need to rely more so on your ears and what you hear. The same is true for a self-driving car. If the cameras are obscured due to snow and sleet, it might be that the radar can provide a greater indication of what the external conditions consist of.

In the case of a self-driving car, there can be a plethora of such sensory devices. Each is reporting what it can. Each might have its difficulties. Each might have its limitations, such as how far ahead it can detect an object. All of these limitations need to be considered during the sensor fusion task.

D-03: Virtual World Model

For humans, we presumably keep in our minds a model of the world around us when we are driving a car. In your mind, you know that the car is going at say 60 miles per hour and that you are on a freeway. You have a model in your mind that your car is surrounded by other cars, and that there are lanes to the freeway. Your model is not only based on what you can see, hear, etc., but also what you know about the nature of the world. You know that at any moment that car ahead of you can smash on its brakes, or the car behind you can ram into your car, or that the truck in the next lane might swerve into your lane.

The AI of the self-driving car needs to have a virtual world model, which it then keeps updated with whatever it is receiving from the sensor fusion, which received its input from the sensor capture and the sensory devices.

D-04: System Action Plan

By having a virtual world model, the AI of the self-driving car is able to keep track of where the car is and what is happening around the car. In addition, the AI needs to determine what to do next. Should the self-driving car hit its brakes? Should the self-driving car stay in its lane or swerve into the lane to the left? Should the self-driving car accelerate or slow down?

A system action plan needs to be prepared by the AI of the self-driving car. The action plan specifies what actions should be taken. The actions need to pertain to the status of the virtual world model. Plus, the actions need to be realizable.

This realizability means that the AI cannot just assert that the self-driving car should suddenly sprout wings and fly. Instead, the AI must be bound by whatever the self-driving car can actually do, such as coming to a halt in a distance of X feet at a speed of Y miles per hour, rather than perhaps asserting that the self-driving car come to a halt in 0 feet as though it could instantaneously come to a stop while it is in motion.

D-05: Controls Activation

The system action plan is implemented by activating the controls of the car to act according to what the plan stipulates. This might mean that the accelerator control is commanded to increase the speed of the car. Or, the steering control is commanded to turn the steering wheel 30 degrees to the left or right.

One question arises as to whether or not the controls respond as they are commanded to do. In other words, suppose the AI has commanded the accelerator to increase, but for some reason it does not do so. Or, maybe it tries to do so, but the speed of the car does not increase. The controls activation feeds back into the virtual world model, and simultaneously the virtual world model is getting updated from the sensors, the sensor capture, and the sensor fusion. This allows the AI to ascertain what has taken place as a result of the controls being commanded to take some kind of action.

By the way, please keep in mind that though the diagram seems to have a linear progression to it, the reality is that these are all aspects of the self-driving car that are happening in parallel and simultaneously. The sensors are capturing data, meanwhile the sensor fusion is taking place, meanwhile the virtual model is being updated, meanwhile the system action plan is being formulated and reformulated, meanwhile the controls are being activated.

This is the same as a human being that is driving a car. They are eyeballing the road, meanwhile they are fusing in their mind the sights, sounds, etc., meanwhile their mind is updating their model of the world around them, meanwhile they are formulating an action plan of what to do, and meanwhile they are pushing their foot onto the pedals and steering the car. In the normal course of driving a car, you are doing all of these at once. I mention this so that when you look at the diagram, you will think of the boxes as processes that are all happening at the same time, and not as though only one happens and then the next.

They are shown diagrammatically in a simplistic manner to help comprehend what is taking place. You though should also realize that they are working in parallel and simultaneous with each other. This is a tough aspect in that the inter-element communications involve latency and other aspects that must be taken into account. There can be delays in one element updating and then sharing its latest status with other elements.

D-06: Automobile & CAN

Contemporary cars use various automotive electronics and a Controller Area Network (CAN) to serve as the components that underlie the driving aspects of a car. There are Electronic Control Units (ECU's) which control subsystems of the car, such as the engine, the brakes, the doors, the windows, and so on.

The elements D-01, D-02, D-03, D-04, D-05 are layered on top of the D-06, and must be aware of the nature of what the D-06 is able to do and not do.

D-07: In-Car Commands

Humans are going to be occupants in self-driving cars. In a Level 5 self-driving car, there must be some form of communication that takes place between the humans and the self-driving car. For example, I go into a self-driving car and tell it that I want to be driven over to Disneyland, and along the way I want to stop at In-and-Out Burger. The self-driving car now parses what I've said and tries to then establish a means to carry out my wishes.

In-car commands can happen at any time during a driving journey. Though my example was about an in-car command when I first got into my self-driving car, it could be that while the self-driving car is carrying out the journey that I change my mind. Perhaps after getting stuck in traffic, I tell the self-driving car to forget about getting the burgers and just head straight over to the theme park. The self-driving car needs to be alert to in-car commands throughout the journey.

D-08: VX2 Communications

We will ultimately have self-driving cars communicating with each other, doing so via V2V (Vehicle-to-Vehicle) communications. We will also have self-driving cars that communicate with the roadways and other aspects of the transportation infrastructure, doing so via V2I (Vehicle-to-Infrastructure).

The variety of ways in which a self-driving car will be communicating with other cars and infrastructure is being called V2X, whereby the letter X means whatever else we identify as something that a car should or would want to communicate with. The V2X communications will be taking place simultaneous with everything else on the diagram, and those other elements will need to incorporate whatever it gleans from those V2X communications.

D-09: Deep Learning

The use of Deep Learning permeates all other aspects of the self-driving car. The AI of the self-driving car will be using deep learning to do a better job at the systems action plan, and at the controls activation, and at the sensor fusion, and so on.

Currently, the use of artificial neural networks is the most prevalent form of deep learning. Based on large swaths of data, the neural networks attempt to "learn" from the data and therefore direct the efforts of the self-driving car accordingly.

D-10: Tactical AI

Tactical AI is the element of dealing with the moment-to-moment driving of the self-driving car. Is the self-driving car staying in its lane of the freeway? Is the car responding appropriately to the controls commands? Are the sensory devices working?

For human drivers, the tactical equivalent can be seen when you watch a novice driver such as a teenager that is first driving. They are focused on the mechanics of the driving task, keeping their eye on the road while also trying to properly control the car.

D-11: Strategic AI

The Strategic AI aspects of a self-driving car are dealing with the larger picture of what the self-driving car is trying to do. If I had asked that the self-driving car take me to Disneyland, there is an overall journey map that needs to be kept and maintained.

There is an interaction between the Strategic AI and the Tactical AI. The Strategic AI is wanting to keep on the mission of the driving, while the Tactical AI is focused on the particulars underway in the driving effort. If the Tactical AI seems to wander away from the overarching mission, the Strategic AI wants to see why and get things back on track. If the Tactical AI realizes that there is something amiss on the self-driving car, it needs to alert the Strategic AI accordingly and have an adjustment to the overarching mission that is underway.

D-12: Self-Aware AI

Very few of the self-driving cars being developed are including a Self-Aware AI element, which we at the Cybernetic Self-Driving Car Institute believe is crucial to Level 5 self-driving cars.

The Self-Aware AI element is intended to watch over itself, in the sense that the AI is making sure that the AI is working as intended. Suppose you had a human driving a car, and they were starting to drive erratically. Hopefully, their own self-awareness would make them realize they themselves are driving poorly, such as perhaps starting to fall asleep after having been driving for hours on end. If you had a passenger in the car, they might be able to alert the driver if the driver is starting to do something amiss. This is exactly what the Self-Aware

AI element tries to do, it becomes the overseer of the AI, and tries to detect when the AI has become faulty or confused, and then find ways to overcome the issue.

D-13: Economic

The economic aspects of a self-driving car are not per se a technology aspect of a self-driving car, but the economics do indeed impact the nature of a self-driving car. For example, the cost of outfitting a self-driving car with every kind of possible sensory device is prohibitive, and so choices need to be made about which devices are used. And, for those sensory devices chosen, whether they would have a full set of features or a more limited set of features.

We are going to have self-driving cars that are at the low-end of a consumer cost point, and others at the high-end of a consumer cost point. You cannot expect that the self-driving car at the low-end is going to be as robust as the one at the high-end. I realize that many of the self-driving car pundits are acting as though all self-driving cars will be the same, but they won't be. Just like anything else, we are going to have self-driving cars that have a range of capabilities. Some will be better than others. Some will be safer than others. This is the way of the real-world, and so we need to be thinking about the economics aspects when considering the nature of self-driving cars.

D-14: Societal

This component encompasses the societal aspects of AI which also impacts the technology of self-driving cars. For example, the famous Trolley Problem involves what choices should a self-driving car make when faced with life-and-death matters. If the self-driving car is about to either hit a child standing in the roadway, or instead ram into a tree at the side of the road and possibly kill the humans in the self-driving car, which choice should be made?

We need to keep in mind the societal aspects will underlie the AI of the self-driving car. Whether we are aware of it explicitly or not, the AI will have embedded into it various societal assumptions.

D-15: Innovation

I included the notion of innovation into the framework because we can anticipate that whatever a self-driving car consists of, it will continue to be innovated over time. The self-driving cars coming out in the next several years will undoubtedly be different and less innovative than the versions that come out in ten years hence, and so on.

Framework Overall

For those of you that want to learn about self-driving cars, you can potentially pick a particular element and become specialized in that aspect. Some engineers are focusing on the sensory devices. Some engineers focus on the controls activation. And so on. There are specialties in each of the elements.

Researchers are likewise specializing in various aspects. For example, there are researchers that are using Deep Learning to see how best it can be used for sensor fusion. There are other researchers that are using Deep Learning to derive good System Action Plans. Some are studying how to develop AI for the Strategic aspects of the driving task, while others are focused on the Tactical aspects.

A well-prepared all-around software developer that is involved in self-driving cars should be familiar with all of the elements, at least to the degree that they know what each element does. This is important since whatever piece of the pie that the software developer works on, they need to be knowledgeable about what the other elements are doing.

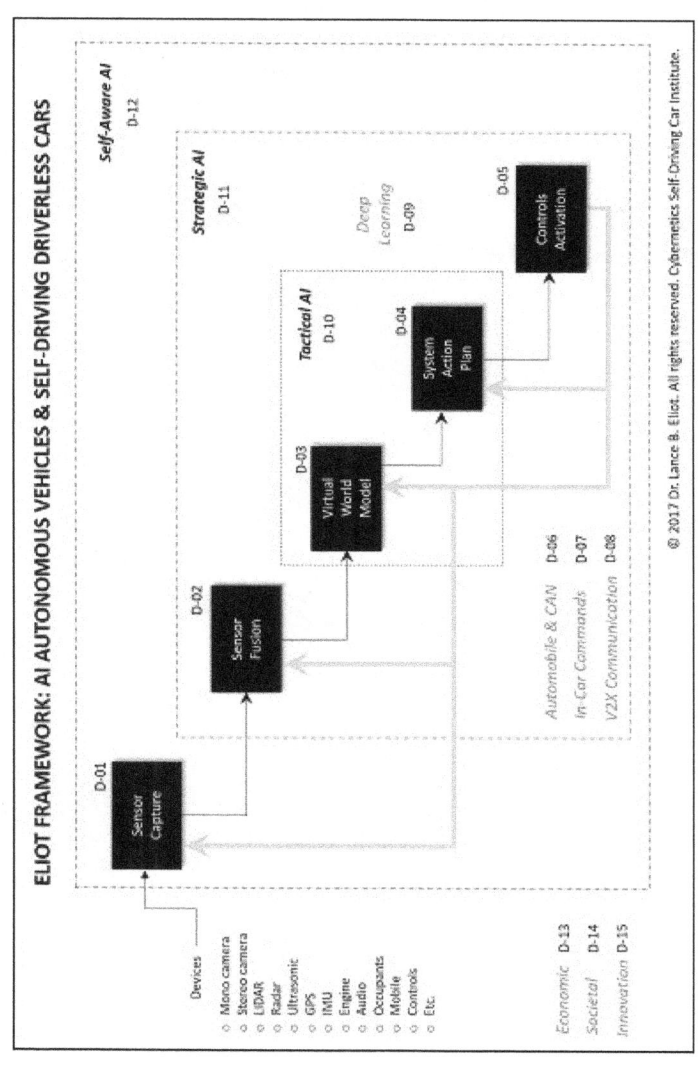

CHAPTER 2

MANEUVERABILITY AND SELF-DRIVING CARS

CHAPTER 2

MANEUVERABILITY AND SELF-DRIVING CARS

Float like a butterfly, sting like a bee.

You might remember or have heard this famous quote which was uttered by Muhammad Ali in 1964. He was referring to his boxing prowess at the time. He was young (age 22) and a boxer that delighted in being on his toes and weaving and bobbing around the boxing ring. Able to be as agile as a butterfly, he could move so readily and quickly that it was hard for his opponents to land a punch. This clever turn of a phrase has become legendary and used whenever someone wants to claim they are agile and fast.

Driving a car is somewhat the same.

Novice drivers are slow to react and often drive a car as though it is a Sherman tank. You've likely sat behind a student driver while on the highway or on a crowded city street. If so, you know how exasperating it can be. The learning driver will start and stop, sometimes for no apparent reason. They will take curves at an agonizingly slow pace, typically an inch at a time. They often hog the road and make it hard to get around them. They are the opposite of a butterfly. Maybe one could say they are more akin to an elephant, lumbering and causing traffic around them to bunch up and slow down.

One especially noticeable aspect of the novice driver is that they tend to pick a lane and stay with it, until they are pretty much forced to change to a different lane. This makes sense in that it is easier to just drive along in a particular lane, and from their viewpoint switching lanes is overly tricky. To switch a lane you need to gauge the traffic in your lane and the lane you want to go into. You are supposed to signal and wait for the right moment to make the switching move. You need to guide the car into the other lane and do so without steering into another car. You need to watch your speed. You need to keep from hitting the car ahead of you. You need to keep from getting hit by another car. And on, and on.

Proficient drivers scoff as this kind of a maneuver in the sense that it is easy for them to pull it off. They cannot imagine why a novice driver has so much trouble changing a lane. For gosh sakes, it's just a lane change, the proficient driver exclaims. No big deal. But, if you ask a novice driver, they will tell you about the nightmares they have of dreading making lane changes. The need to pay attention to so many variables simultaneously that it is mentally overloading. The danger factor is extremely high and they realize that one wrong move and it could be a bad day for them and everyone else involved. I've seen some novice drivers that never reach a sufficient proficiency level and pretty much stay off the highway because they want to avoid fast-speed lane changing.

Maneuvering a car is easy to speak of, but doing it successfully requires building up an appropriate skill.

Go back in time to when you first drove a car, and I'm betting you'll be able to remember the cold sweats when you were first sat behind the wheel of a car. It's a huge responsibility. You will determine the fate of the car, your own life is now in your hands, and the lives of any occupants in your car are in your hands, as are the drivers and occupants of other cars that you'll come across while driving. Pedestrians lives are in your hands. Dogs and cats lives are in your hands. In whatever manner you decide to maneuver the car, you can either hit, injure, or kill living things. Most of us drive our cars every day and don't think overtly about any of this. Instead, we just take it for granted that we have in our hands the destiny of those around us.

Over time, a savvy novice driver should be improving in the skills at maneuvering a car. They gradually learn how to go more quickly around curves. They progressively get more comfortable switching lanes. They adjust mentally and learn new tricks of driving. Driving becomes less of a conscious skill and begins to come naturally. The car becomes an extension of their own arms and legs. There is a flow of sorts that happens and the car and the driver become one. I know this sounds like some kind of zen thing, but I am just saying that the novice driver becomes more comfortable in the driving role and eventually settles into it.

Even proficient drivers though can be shocked back into the reality of how difficult it is to maneuver a car successfully. A colleague of mine that drives a nice sports car is continually bragging about how he can zoom around in traffic. He tells tall tales about how he was able to get to work in record time by "scaring the sheep" drivers and having them get out of his way (he aims his car at other cars, and plays a game of chicken to get them out-of-his-way – a dangerous and foolhardy gambit). Well, one day, he got into a car accident, which fortunately no one was seriously hurt, but he was taken aback and suddenly remarked that maybe he was cutting corners a bit too much. The NASCAR cockiness for a moment had receded and he had a realization that cars are large physical objects with a potential for harming him and others. He had forgotten this.

It turns out that maneuverability is a topic that has been studied closely by animal behaviorists. A recent interesting study examined how hummingbirds are able to be so nimble. In the study, computer vision systems were used to record and analyze the movements of more than 200 hummingbirds. We are all familiar with how agile hummingbirds are, and they seem to shift direction on a dime. What is the morphology that explains this capability? The analysis showed that it is a combination of the shape of their wings and as combined with their skills. These marvelous creatures are able to rapidly fuse together sensory data about their environment, and use it to then avoid obstacles and do so at incredibly breakneck speeds.

The study included 25 different species of hummingbirds. Certain of the species would use one kind of maneuvers, while a different species would choose to use a different set. Aspects such as forward acceleration and deceleration were largely determined by muscular capacity. Wing shape and size made it either easy, or hard, for making particular kinds of maneuvers. Diversity in their ability to fly raises questions of why not just have the same capability for all hummingbirds. It is thought that evolutionary factors ultimately led to different variants, and each distinct set of factors then leads to a hummingbird that is best suited for its environmental niche.

When you translate this study of hummingbirds over to the domain of cars, you can consider that the physical aspect of the car determines some of the maneuverability aspects, akin to how the shape and size of a hummingbird wing determines the limits of what maneuvers can be made. With hummingbirds, it's more than just their physical shape, since they also need to perceive their environment and their brains need to engage as to how their bodies are to react. Likewise, when driving a car, the human driver needs to mentally gather sensory information, fuse it together, and cognitively make decisions in real-time to control the car.

For a car, the size of the car is one determiner of maneuverability. Think about a subcompact sized car versus the maneuverability of a giant sized SUV. How fast does the car go from zero to 60 miles per hour? What kind of tires does the car have, just normal traction or high-performance tires? There are numerous physical aspects about a car that determine what kind of maneuverability it can potentially have. In the end, it is the mind and hands of the driver that will showcase the physical maneuverability of the car. A novice driver tends to drive all cars the same way, and has not yet learned how to leverage the potential maneuverability of the car. A proficient driver is able to ascertain what the car can do, and has the capability to make use of the car's proficiencies.

The environment surrounding a car will also significantly shape the maneuverability options. If it is raining and the roads are slick, a car that could normally do the zero to 60 miles per hour in 4.4 seconds on a dry road is unlikely to be able to do so on a wet road, even if the human driver is highly proficient. The physics of the road conditions and the car will provide limits on what the human driver can do.

Besides the weather and the roadway, there's also the factor of traffic. If you are in a superfast car that has incredible maneuverability, and suppose you are the top car racer in the world, but if you are on the Los Angeles 405 freeway at 5:00 p.m. on a weekday, when the freeway is completely clogged with cars and its stop-and-go at less than 5 miles per hour, your keen maneuverability skills and car capabilities will be stymied.

Allow me to add another factor into driving maneuverability. I mentioned earlier about my colleague that bragged about his driving prowess and used bulldog tactics to get his way. I'm going to suggest that we consider driving maneuverability to include something that he does not exhibit, namely being able to drive with grace and aplomb. I say that because mindless darting into and out of lanes does not make for a highly successful sense of maneuverability. Any clod can do that. A truly maneuverable-capable driver is able to maneuver in such a manner that they have a neutral or even positive impact on the rest of the traffic around them.

Say what? I am sure some of you are perplexed by my claim. Allow me to further elaborate. If you are maneuvering a car in traffic and able to get where you want to go, efficiently and effectively, and simultaneously avoid negatively impacting other traffic, you are doing maneuverability the way it is intended to properly be done. In contrast, the sloppy and careless maneuverable driver is one that makes lane changes at the last moment and forces other cars to jam on their brakes. These low-skilled maneuvers are done in a fashion that increases the risks and danger of driving for them and the other drivers around them. A successful driver is one that has high maneuverability skills, and for which they combine those skills with the nature of the maneuverability of the car and the maneuverability allowed by the nature of the roadway environmental conditions.

What does this have to do with AI self-driving cars?

At the Cybernetic Self-Driving Car Institute, we are developing AI that enables self-driving cars to drive with a high degree of successful maneuverability. They are like hummingbirds.

You might be wondering, well, Lance, won't all self-driving cars be designed and developed with AI for a high degree of successful maneuverability? The answer, right now, is no. Currently, most of the auto makers and tech firms are zipping ahead with getting their self-driving cars on the roadways and the "clod" approach to driving is just fine, they believe.

If you observe how today's AI self-driving cars maneuver, you would realize quickly that they are driving like a novice. They get into a lane, and hesitate to get out of the lane. When they switch lanes, it's done only in the safest of circumstances and the self-driving car acts very timidly. The maneuverability factor is low, in terms of the driver. It's not the car, since the cars are generally the same kinds of cars that we humans drive. It's the AI that's not up to par.

We want to have AI that can drive a car as a proficient human would drive a car. A Level 5 self-driving car is one that can be driven by the AI and does not need any human intervention. The self-driving car industry is not yet at a Level 5 self-driving car, nobody has achieved it. Even once we get there, the Level 5 criteria does not explicitly say how good a driver the AI must be. In other words, you could have a clod of an AI driver. But, is that what we all in our hearts want a Level 5 to truly be?

AI self-driving cars are going to be mixing with human driven cars for quite some time. Let's suppose that the first round of AI self-driving cars at the Level 5 are all clod drivers. In that sense, none of them are very good at maneuverability. When they make driving maneuvers, it is stilted and tends to adversely impact the rest of traffic. This is going to be a dangerous situation. Imagine that we have say 50 human driven cars on a stretch of freeway, and we mix into it 10 of the AI self-driving cars that are driving like novices. The odds are that you're going to have human driven cars that will have a difficult time dealing with this many novices all at once.

We are used to having a few student drivers mixed into traffic, but not have them be say 10% of the traffic, or 30% of the traffic, or half of the traffic. It's a recipe for disaster. I realize the utopian view of self-driving cars is that the world will consist of only self-driving cars. This is nonsense. We cannot overnight replace 200 million conventional cars (in the United States) and suddenly have all self-driving cars. Some have said that we should have special lanes on our roadways that are dedicated to self-driving cars, and not allow human driven cars to mix in with them. This has a steep price in terms of altering our roadways to do this, plus there will be angry debates about whether this is allowing the privileged (those able to afford self-driving cars) to have something that the rest of the populace cannot readily have.

Let me repeat my earlier statement about driving: A truly maneuverable-capable driver is able to maneuver in such a manner that they have a neutral or even positive impact on the rest of the traffic around them. Now, let's insert into the sentence that the driver is AI.

Thus, here's the modern version:

A truly maneuverable-capable AI self-driving car is able to maneuver in such a manner that it will have a neutral or even positive impact on the rest of the traffic around them.

It's not enough to just make a maneuver. The maneuver not only needs to be safe, but also must be done with a perspective on the impact to the rest of the traffic. The desired impact is either neutral or positive. The undesirable impact is one that is negative.

Here's a traffic example to illustrate.

Imagine you are in a lane of traffic. The car is going at 50 miles per hour. You want to change lanes into the lane to your right. There is an available gap in traffic in that lane. You can make the lane change, legally, and without hitting another car. Seems easy. Just go ahead and change lanes.

Suppose that I tell you that in the lane that's to your right, there's a car coming up in that lane. It's not yet reached being parallel to your car, and so there is still a physical gap for you to move into the lane. That car though is moving at 65 miles per hour. It is rapidly closing the open gap. If you move into the lane, it will force that other driver to hit their brakes to the degree that they need to rapidly decelerate their car.

I think we would all agree that any driver that jumped into another lane, and forced an upcoming driver to have to rapidly hit their brakes, would be taking a dicey maneuver. Yes, you could say that the other driver should be watching for a car that jumps into their lane. Yes, you could say that the other driver should let in that car. But, I think it's relatively evident that if the first car caused the second car to hit their brakes, and suppose that behind that second car there was another third car that now had to hit its brakes, the first car has started a cascade of negative impacts on fellow traffic.

Most of today's AI self-driving cars are driving on the roadways and playing a chess game whereby they only are looking at their most immediate move. Can you move the rook into that open space on the chessboard? Yes, but then the next move after that will allow the queen to take your king. AI self-driving cars are not yet looking ahead of their next move and figuring out the consequences of the moves. They are one ply (meaning looking at a single move), rather than say three ply or five ply (looking ahead by three or five moves).

The AI needs to be using the sensor data to anticipate the adverse impacts on traffic due to the maneuvers potentially to be made by the self-driving car. As part of the sensor fusion and virtual model updating, the AI needs to be planning for what will happen if any given move X is going to be attempted. Can the AI self-driving car maneuver into the lane to the right, and if it does so, will it cut off other traffic? Will it create a cascading set of car collisions or issues? This is what must be done to be a proficient driver of a self-driving car.

For some auto makers and tech firms, they are using large datasets of driving data to train the AI via the use of neural networks to be able to find patterns of driving and act accordingly. This can be handy, but it can also be narrow in that it only is examining the data being provided. If you fed it data of cars changing lanes, and you did not include the consequent traffic repercussions, you would essentially be training the AI to be a clod driver. It is crucial that the datasets of driving data be sufficiently robust to enable the neural network to be aware of a large enough picture of the roadway and road conditions.

Ultimately, we want the AI to float like a butterfly, and not sting like a bee. Efforts toward making AI that is a proficient driver, one with a degree of successful maneuverability, must be a key goal for all self-driving car makers.

CHAPTER 3

COMMON SENSE REASONING AND SELF-DRIVING CARS

CHAPTER 3

COMMON SENSE REASONING AND SELF-DRIVING CARS

What is common sense?

There was a story in the news the other day about a man that got his arm stuck in a toilet while trying to reach in and fish out his smartphone that he had dropped into the privy. Some immediately said he had no common sense. What person with any common sense would reach down so far that they would get their arm stuck?

Well, I suppose we could consider whether something like this has ever been taught in school. Probably not (I don't recall in K-12 ever being told to not put an arm down inside the privy). How was he supposed to know that he should not take such action? Perhaps knowing not to do this is actually uncommon knowledge and so why do we assume it falls within the realm of common sense?

I am guessing that you likely believe it farfetched to think that a grown man would not realize the potential for getting his arm stuck in such a situation, and that in spite of the topic never being covered in classes, it just stands to reason that trying to reach down too far is bound to be a bad idea. Plus of course there's the yuk factor involved in it too.

Let's try a different angle on the topic of common sense.

Suppose you go to an obscure country and go hiking. You see a very pretty flower. You decide to go ahead and touch the flower, and even take some of the flowers with you. A few minutes after handling the flower, your hands and arms begin to show signs of a rash. Within an hour, you are dealing with itching hives all over most of your body. What happened? You opted to grab hold of a toxic flower. Locals see you and immediately know what you've done. They shake their heads and think that there's another tourist lacking in common sense!

Was this awareness about grabbing the flower indeed a common-sense matter? Some would say that they had no idea that such a flower was toxic and so it isn't right to characterize it as common sense. But, if that's the case, what about the man that jammed his arm in the privy?

Defining what we mean by common sense can be somewhat problematic. For example, common sense can be culturally based, such as the instance of the toxic flower whereby those that lived in that culture and region all knew about the flower, while you as a tourist did not. Common sense can also vary over time, in the sense that if you go back in history, there are things a hundred years ago that people of that time period would say is common sense, and yet today we might not know at all.

Can common sense be learned? Some say that it is not learned explicitly and that you just somehow gain it implicitly. For little children, we teach them to not put their hand on a hot stove. You could assert that this is a form of explicitly learned common sense. You can't normally lift an entire car by yourself, but do we explicitly teach children this? Do we have children go to a car and try to lift it? Not usually. Instead, the child learns that heavy objects cannot be lifted by their own strength alone, and they realize that a car is a heavy object. You might say that in this case the common sense about lifting a car is based on implicit learning.

Learning about things involves generalizing from what has been learned. The case of the child that learned about heavy objects and then generalized that this applies to cars too, it showcases that we don't need to learn about everything in the world per se and can learn something that we can apply to other circumstances. This though can go awry. There is a famous case of a child that was scared by a white furred dog, and the child then became fearful of any animal that was white in color. Was this the proper kind of generalization? No. This was a form of generalization that was based on a faulty kind of thinking.

Does intelligence include common sense?

If we say that someone is highly intelligent, do we also simultaneously mean that they have a hefty common sense? I am sure that you likely know some geniuses that at times appear to exhibit very little common sense. Indeed, our society appears to accept the idea that someone that we consider having a very high IQ is likely to actually lack common sense (you might think of Sheldon in The Big Bang Theory as a portrayal of this). It's as though we believe that their minds are so occupied with the tough stuff that those geniuses have little mental space for and little regard for the more mundane things that we pile into the rubric of common sense.

Even those high IQ people still though have some amount of common sense, since they appear to operate sufficiently in the real-world and know things that we might consider to be common sense. For example, we seem to know that you can't be in two places at the same time. That's just common sense, most would say, and I would claim that even the highest IQ person would know this too. In other words, we might joke that a certain person has "no common sense" but we are really exaggerating by using the word "no" and that they indeed have some amount of common sense. Their common sense might be spotty, and they get themselves on occasion into a bad spot, including reaching too far into a toilet, but nonetheless they do have a modicum of common sense.

We might then agree that intelligence does include common sense. A person can be low in intelligence or high in intelligence, and they can be low in common sense or they can be high in common sense. Whichever way it goes, there is going to be both intelligence and common sense. We can quibble about whether intelligence includes common sense, or whether they are colleagues of each other and neither is subsumed by the other. Anyway, let's go with the notion that with intelligence there is also some amount of common sense.

AI is Lacking in Common Sense

For purposes of developing Artificial Intelligence (AI), we need to figure out what is meant by "intelligence" since we are trying to develop automated systems that do that same thing. As such, if in fact common sense is integral to intelligence, presumably when creating an AI system we would also intend to have it embody common sense. Without embodying common sense, we would be developing something that is less than what we would consider as intelligent and it would lack what might be considered as a vital piece of that puzzle.

Right now, most AI systems lack any semblance of common sense.

Indeed, in the AI field there is regular AI and there is AGI, which stands for Artificial General Intelligence. The AGI is considered the kind of AI that includes common sense reasoning. To-date, AI systems have been devoted to specialized tasks and have not had to contain common sense. Some say that these are weak forms of AI, and that a strong form of AI would embody common sense. Do we need common sense in AI to do specialized tasks? There are those that say you don't need common sense in specialized areas, since the task is whittled down to something that only needs specialized knowledge and no common sense is required.

What does this have to do with AI self-driving cars?

At the Cybernetic Self-Driving Car Institute, we are developing AI systems for self-driving cars and also exploring the inclusion of common sense reasoning.

The existing AI systems for self-driving cars don't have common sense reasoning. Instead, they are systems devoted to the task of driving, and it is claimed that driving does not need common sense. There is controversy over that claim. Is it that driving does not need common sense or is it that since we haven't reached a point of being able to truly develop artificial common sense that we are simply OK with saying that it isn't needed for the task of driving. You be the judge.

Thus, we have these options:

- Common sense is not needed at all for AI self-driving cars

- Common sense would be a nice-to-have for AI self-driving cars but isn't required

- Common sense is a necessity for AI self-driving cars

If you believe that common sense is not needed at all for AI self-driving cars, you are akin to many AI developers that would say the same thing. If you are in the boat of saying that it would be a nice-to-have, I believe that many in the AI field would say sure, it would be nice to have, but they also would say it would be nice to be the king of the world, and so there are lots of things that would be nice to have. Why worry about something that's just nice to have, they would say.

If you believe that common sense is a necessity for AI self-driving cars, you might be concerned that there are few efforts afoot to embody common sense into the AI for self-driving cars. There are some that think we won't be able to achieve true self-driving cars, ones at Level 5, which are intended to be able to drive a car as a human would, unaided by a human driver, without a breakthrough in common sense reasoning. Those that think this are relatively few, and others in AI would scoff at them. No need to wait for common sense reasoning to be perfected, they say, and let's just keep plowing forward on driving as a specialized task that does not require common sense.

How Much Common Sense Is Required To Drive?

Suppose though that common-sense reasoning is the secret ingredient that makes AI self-driving cars truly possible. You might argue that 90% of the task of driving does not need common sense and that it's only a paltry 10%. Excuse me, but if you are having self-driving cars on the road that are supposed to be true self-driving cars, and if they are missing 10% of what they need to know, I don't think we'd be satisfied with the end result. This implies that the AI of the self-driving cars won't be able to fully perform the task at hand. I realize some might say it's more like 99% for specialized knowledge and maybe 1% for common sense, but even this is still something to raise your eyebrows. If we ultimately take all 200+ million conventional cars in the United States alone and replace them eventually with all AI self-driving cars, are you willing to deal with the 1% of the time that involves them from not being able to properly perform the driving task in certain circumstances?

For those of you that recall AI efforts in the 1980s, you might remember the big hullabaloo that occurred about the need to achieve common sense reasoning. A consortium known as MCC, consisting of some of the biggest tech firms of the era, poured a ton of money into seeking common sense reasoning. Those of you that lived through that period will remember the common-sense engine Cyc, which got government funding and private funding. The idea was to codify all the simple truths of life, incorporating thousands upon thousands of common sense rules. Believe it or not, the Cyc effort still continues today (based on the tenacity of Doug Lenat), having rules into the millions, and there have been efforts to try and commercialize it. There are other similar kinds of efforts, such as the laudable work being done at AI2, the Allen Institute for AI, a bold effort by Paul Allen.

Seasoned AI developers and researchers are bound to say that they thought we left common sense reasoning efforts long ago. They are forgotten relics today, they say. Those efforts appeared to be an errand for fool's gold, and at the time many were irked that monies flowed to something that was a seemingly insurmountable task. There were suggestions that it would take 350 human-years to achieve a common-sense reasoning capability. It takes some guts to be willing to persist on an endeavor that won't have a substantial payoff for that length of time.

Over time, there have been heated arguments about whether it makes sense to try and codify common sense into individual rules. You can't be in more than one place at a time. You can't lift a heavy car. You shouldn't put your arm down deep into a privy. It would seem that we would have a nearly endless list of such rules. How can you capture all of those rules? Suppose there aren't just millions of such rules, but maybe billions or more? Furthermore, as mentioned earlier, common sense changes over time and thus whatever you consider to be common sense now might be outdated or need to be supplemented with newer common sense. It seems to have an endless scope and one that we can't even figure out where the boundaries of the scope is.

In fact, some would say that forget about trying to do things the brute force way. Rather than trying to find all of these individual rules and codify them into a system, we might instead use machine learning to ferret out the aspects of common sense. If you use an artificial neural network to pattern on data, presumably it will pick-up the nature of the common-sense reasoning that is otherwise hidden within the data. Maybe children don't actually learn common sense by individual rules, and instead their minds see the world around them and via neuronal patterning they come to gain common sense. It could be that we falsely turn these into individual rules, simply because its easier for us to explain what logically seems to be occurring, but in fact it might be a misleading representation of what actually is happening in the mind.

If you believe in the notion that common sense arises as a matter of course in the dense fabric of neuronal activity, you would likely be even more dubious about efforts to by-hand create artificial common sense by the entering of simplistic rules. Those that believe in the by-hand creation say that we just need more ways to do the by-hand codification. Perhaps we should do more crowdsourcing of the by-hand approach. Let's get all 7.6 billion people on this planet and get them to help enter the common-sense rules. Imagine how quickly you might be able to get toward a common-sense reasoning system. This though obviously has numerous logistics issues, technological issues, and would seem a bit farfetched as a viable approach.

You might be thinking about systems like Google's Knowledge Graph or Microsoft's Satori and wondering if this is a sign of our reaching a common-sense reasoning capability. Though those kinds of efforts are encouraging, it's not really what most would describe as an effort toward capturing full common sense reasoning. I assure you, trying to achieve common sense reasoning, whether via the by-hand approach or via the machine learning approach, it's a really tough problem. That you can bet on. There's no magic bullet that seems to be anywhere in sight on this.

Given all this discussion about common sense reasoning, where does it though arise in the driving task? Maybe those that say we don't need it are right. Perhaps there isn't any common-sense reasoning involved in driving a car. If so, you can drop this topic from the AI self-driving car field and instead consider it as an interesting curiosity for the rest of AI.

A few years ago, I went to an event that had only a dirt parking lot for the event and so I parked my car on the dirt. The event itself took place in an indoor venue. I went into the venue and enjoyed the event. Came out to my car a few hours later. During the event, rain had poured down. The dirt had become a muddy mess. I could not get my car out the parking lot, it was stuck in the mud. When I have gone into the venue, I had seen ominous rain clouds. You might say that common sense would have warned me to not park on the dirt, since I could have reasoned that when it rains that dirt turns to mud, and that cars don't normally drive well in the mud.

Do we expect an AI self-driving car to have this kind of common sense reasoning? Should an AI self-driving car be able to consider where you park the self-driving car, and whether or not it is on dirt, and whether or not there is rain forecasted, and whether the self-driving car could get stuck in the mud if the rain turned it the dirt to mud, etc. Some would say this is crazy to consider that we would expect an AI self-driving car to figure this kind of thing out.

Let's try something else. I was driving my car down a neighborhood street that I had not been on before. As I was driving, I noticed that there were three young boys perched on a rooftop of a home along the street. They seemed to be hiding, yet I could see their heads peering over the roofline. They seemed to be staring at the cars going down the street. I decided to make a U-turn, since the situation was odd. As I did so, a car ahead of me approached where the house was. The boys tossed water balloons at the car. This could have created an accident, and everyone was lucky that nothing bad happened per se.

Was it common sense that led me to make the U-turn? Would we expect an AI self-driving car to have that same kind of common sense? You might say that this circumstance is not part of the driving task per se, and that it's an oddball and thus not fair to suggest that an AI system would need to ascertain something like this.

Let's try this. I was driving on the freeway and up ahead I saw a pick-up truck that had a bunch of debris sitting in the bed of the truck. The debris was not covered up and was just sitting there, subject to the wind. I used what I believe to be common sense and figured that at some point that debris might fly out of the bed of the truck. I didn't want to be behind the truck when it might happen. So, I moved over to the next lane. Sure enough, moments later, I saw the truck hit a pothole in the freeway, which bumped the truck enough that some of the debris spilled onto the freeway. The car directly behind the truck swerved wildly to avoid the debris, which then led to other cars all swerving madly.

Presumably, an AI self-driving car would be like those other drivers and have only reacted once the debris hit the roadway. Would we expect an AI self-driving car to have deduced that debris in the bed of a truck might come loose and fly out of the truck? Is that an obscure notion? I don't think it is an obscure notion and assert it is something that we'd want an AI system to be cognizant of.

One way for the AI to have anticipated this would be if it had experienced it before. Suppose the AI self-driving car was caught in that circumstance, hopefully it would subsequently update itself to anticipate such occurrences in the future. Furthermore, if the AI self-driving car is connected to a cloud that is being used by the auto maker, this instance could go into the cloud, and at some point, all other of the AI self-driving cars by that auto maker might benefit from this learned aspect via an OTA (Over The Air) update.

Of course, we also need to consider that whatever is learned from such an instance is not overly generalized. Remember the case of the child that was frightened by a white furry dog and became fearful of any white colored animal? Would the AI of the self-driving cars "learn" that whenever a truck with a bed of debris is detected that it means debris will fall off the truck? In this case, it was due to hitting the pothole. Also, there wasn't any cover or netting over the debris. We need to consider how would the AI be able to use common sense reasoning to generalize this into something practical and not become overly paranoid about all trucks hauling debris.

Notice that I mentioned that if the AI self-driving car experienced this kind of circumstance before, it might have explicitly learned subsequently about what to do. There are the implicit learning aspects too. Do we need to wait until AI self-driving cars have experienced the many myriad of circumstances before it can be ready to spot such situations? Maybe we could include common sense reasoning into the AI self-driving car, allowing it to anticipate situations that it has not necessarily learned explicitly. If we are dependent upon the AI only doing explicit learning, how many millions upon millions of miles of driving on our public roadways will be needed before the AI learns all that it needs to know? And, during the time, are we going to be vulnerable to the AI not having the needed common sense, and thus being a less safe driver than we otherwise want it to be?

Common sense is not an easy matter. We all take it for granted. Embodying common sense reasoning into AI self-driving cars is an open issue and a quite difficult one to solve. Though some will disagree about whether it is a nice-to-have or a necessity, it's safest to suggest it is beyond the realm of not needed and in the realm of desirable.

CHAPTER 4
COGNITION TIMING
AND
SELF-DRIVING CARS

CHAPTER 4

COGNITION TIMING

AND

SELF-DRIVING CARS

How fast can you think?

If I give you a jigsaw puzzle and ask you to assemble it, you would likely take some amount of time to look at the puzzle pieces and mull over in your mind which piece might go where. You might create a kind of mental picture of how the pieces could potentially fit together. Even before you pick-up a single piece, you might have done a lot of mental calculations and cranial contortions about the pieces and the overall jigsaw puzzle.

Suppose there are just ten pieces to the jigsaw puzzle. Imagine how long it would take for you to mentally envision how those ten pieces will fit together. In contrast, suppose I give you a jigsaw puzzle of 100 pieces, or 1,000 pieces? I'm betting that the amount of mental calculus would go up for those larger-sized jigsaw puzzles.

Suppose further that I give you a jigsaw puzzle that is a picture of farm and has distinctive features such as the farmhouse, cows, horses, and the like. This would tend to make it easier to spot which jigsaw pieces go toward what part of the puzzle. On the other hand, if I gave you a jigsaw puzzle that is all blue in color, and thus there's nothing distinctive about what it portrays, you would find yourself likely struggling to figure out where the jigsaw pieces go.

All of these variable factors about the jigsaw puzzle will tend toward having you use more mental calculations or less mental calculations, and it will correspondingly cause you to spend more time or less time while trying to put together the jigsaw puzzle. Your mental calculations require the consumption of time. If I force you into a situation wherein you need to do more and more mental calculations, it would to some proportional degree increase the time required for you to solve the mental aspects of the puzzle.

I might sit you down in a room and ask you to do a jigsaw puzzle. In so doing, I might tell you that you have as much time as you need. Take your time, I tell you. In that case, assuming you don't have to rush to the dentist or have some other upcoming time-based obligation, you could spend minutes or maybe even hours on the puzzle.

Let's for the moment subtract from the time consumed the "non-mental" time that involves moving the physical pieces. I realize this is somewhat argumentative to suggest that there aren't mental calculations going on while you are moving the pieces, and indeed the reality would be that you likely would be still thinking about the pieces as you move them, but let's just focus for now on the mental time that involves none of the physical manipulation of the puzzle.

Solving the Puzzle with Time Constraints

OK, so there you are, solving this jigsaw puzzle. But, instead of having told you that you can take as much time as you like, suppose I said that you have ten minutes to solve it. Not one second more than ten minutes. If this puzzle seems like it might take more than ten minutes to solve, you would begin to more urgently try to solve the puzzle. You might take less mental breaks. You might take greater chances and your level of concentration might go up (versus a more leisurely mental concentration when you knew that you had unlimited time).

Let's add more pressure. I tell you that you have just ten minutes, and that if you can complete the entire puzzle in the ten minutes that I will give you a million dollars. Whoa! You are suddenly really motivated to solve that puzzle. Your concentration might go up even more so. This is a chance of a lifetime.

The opportunity to win the money was a positive kind of reward. Let's take a different tack. If you don't solve the puzzle in ten minutes, your chair falls through a trapdoor into a pit below and you are a goner. Don't want to get into something untoward here, and I am just trying to suggest that your perspective on the situation might change if you knew it was a life-and-death matter. Would you still be using your same mind and doing the same overall mental calculations? It would seem so. Would you be rushing those mental calculations? It would seem so.

The life-and-death pressure might actually harm your ability to think and solve the puzzle. Often, people discover that in dire situations their mental clarity drops and their mind becomes befuddled. You might also start using your mind to try and find a means to escape from the situation, and as such you are now splitting the use of your mental capacity. Maybe one-third of your mental capacity is on the puzzle, another third on how to escape, and perhaps another third is just in pure panic mode and racing wildly. All in all, this is probably not going to aid you in solving the puzzle. In fact, you might have done better with no pressure or you might have done better with the pressure for the million dollars. Ironically, though solving the puzzle is much more crucial in the life-and-death case, you might do worse mentally.

This discussion about solving the puzzle is an illustration of the cognitive capabilities and effort that we humans have and can make use of. Via your mind, you are able to solve a jigsaw puzzle. Your cognitive efforts take time. Time can be vital to making a mental calculation or decision. We used the time limit of ten minutes to solve the puzzle. In everyday life, you might have to decide which flavor of ice cream to get when at your local creamery and have a minute to figure this out, or you might be a police officer confronting a gunman and you need to mentally decide in a split second whether to fire your gun or not at the assailant.

How do we think?

That's a big question and one that nobody can fully answer as yet. No one has yet cracked open the inner workings of the mind. Step by step, we are all gradually reverse engineering the brain to see how biologically and chemically it works. We can do all kinds of testing and measurements while you are in the process of thinking, but this has not yet fully revealed how cognition really happens. Efforts to reverse engineer mental algorithms are ongoing and it is hoped that someday we'll know exactly how thinking works.

One aspect of cognition is that we seem to be able to undertake cognitive economy when we are aware of the need to do so. Allow me to elaborate on this.

You are told to solve the jigsaw puzzle in ten minutes, and then I cut the time to five minutes. You might be able to adjust your mental processes to be more economical in your thinking, doing so in an effort to cut the needed thinking time to five minutes from ten minutes. Perhaps you opt to examine each jigsaw piece only once, while your normal approach would be to look at each piece twice. Maybe you decide that rather than going deeper in your thinking, you'll do a shallow approach and just move around the pieces based on a hunch or a quicker sense of what to do.

Cognitive Cost Minimization

We seem to be able to do some kind of cognitive cost minimization. We take into account the mental problem to be solved, we consider the amount of time we have, we include the motivation underlying the task, and we then try to shape the nature and amount of cognitive effort accordingly. Now, not everyone seems to do this, or there are many that seem to do a poor job of it. In some cases, it takes specialized training and awareness to realize that you should be doing this kind of cognitive cost minimization.

Little children tend to learn about this aspect without necessarily being explicitly told per se. In kindergarten, they might be given simple tests of guessing at letters of the alphabet or colors on flashcards. They are likely given a limited amount of time to guess. They are motivated to want to do well and appease the teacher and please their parents.

Without explicitly realizing how they are doing it, they are bound to be controlling their minds to become able to do cognitive cost minimization.

What does this have to do with AI self-driving cars?

At the Cybernetic Self-Driving Car Institute, we are developing AI systems for self-driving cars and of which include various means to leverage cognitive economy into these systems.

Cognitive economy for self-driving cars is a life-and-death matter. I'll bet it's something you might not have given much consideration to. A self-driving car is a real-time system, meaning that in real-time things are happening. The AI cannot just leisurely figure out what needs to be done. Akin to my example earlier about solving a jigsaw puzzle in ten minutes, the AI is confronted with the harsh reality of needing to come to decisions and take actions that are at times a split second in nature.

Suppose a self-driving car is driving along on a highway at 40 miles per hour. Up ahead, a pedestrian steps into the street. The AI of the self-driving car has to ascertain what to do. Should the AI instruct the self-driving car to come to a halt? But, if so, how long will it take for the car to come to a halt and will it stop soon enough to keep from hitting the pedestrian? Maybe the AI should tell the self-driving car to swerve and try to avoid hitting the pedestrian.

Setting aside for the moment the physical movements of the car itself, consider the kind of "mental calculations" that the AI needs to do in this situation. It needs to detect where the pedestrian is. It needs to detect how fast the self-driving car is going. It needs to try and predict what will happen in the future, which in this case is the potential collision with the pedestrian. It needs to identify alternative future scenarios such as trying to come to a halt, and figure out whether halting will solve the problem. It needs to identify whether swerving would solve the problem.

All of this is a kind of cognitive effort (not of a human kind, and so please understand that I am using the word cognition for ease of discussion and not to suggest that the AI is thinking in a manner that humans think).

This is a cognitive effort and one that is time bounded. The AI cannot take twenty minutes to derive a viable solution to the problem. It must use whatever limited time is available. As such, the question arises as to how the AI should employ cognitive economy. This could be seen as like trying to solve a chess problem. For chess, you can look at just one move ahead, or two moves ahead, or fifty moves ahead. The more moves ahead you consider (which are called ply), the more time it takes. If you are playing chess and have a three minute per move timer involved, you likely cannot afford to do a fifty moves ahead exploration.

There's the self-driving car, zooming at 40 miles per hour, heading directly toward the pedestrian. The AI has to quickly assess the situation and decide what to do. Pretend that it takes 1 second of time to collect data about the aspect that there's a pedestrian up ahead and in the way, and it takes 1 second of time to consider what actions to take, and another 1 second to issue commands to the car to let's say swerve, and it takes the car 1 second to receive the command and begin the swerving action. That's a total of 4 seconds, just involved in initiating the car to swerve.

A car moving at 40 miles per hour is moving at about 60 feet per second. We have just determined that it will take about 4 seconds to make a decision, and so that means that the car will have moved forward a total of about 240 feet (that's 4 x 60). From an outsider's perspective, the car has seemingly not done anything as yet, in that the AI was "thinking" internally for the four seconds of time. Meanwhile, the car was continuing to barrel forward for the 240 feet.

Suppose I told you that the pedestrian was about 120 feet in front of the self-driving car at the moment when the AI first began its deliberations. Well, sadly, the self-driving car would have plowed into the pedestrian. This is because the AI was still in the process of deciding what to do. The AI had needed the four seconds to figure out what to do, and during that time the self-driving car was like a guided missile continuing on its course and waiting for any new command as to what else to do.

Similar to my story earlier about telling you that you had ten minutes to solve the jigsaw puzzle and then I said that you only had five minutes, the AI of the self-driving car cannot just blindly take whatever amount of time it wants to make a decision, and instead must try to ascertain how much time it does have. And, once it estimates the amount of allowable time, it needs to make use of cognitive economy to try and find a means to make a decision in the shorter allowed time.

Take a look at Figure 1 to see an indication of the stages involved in the AI core processes for a self-driving car.

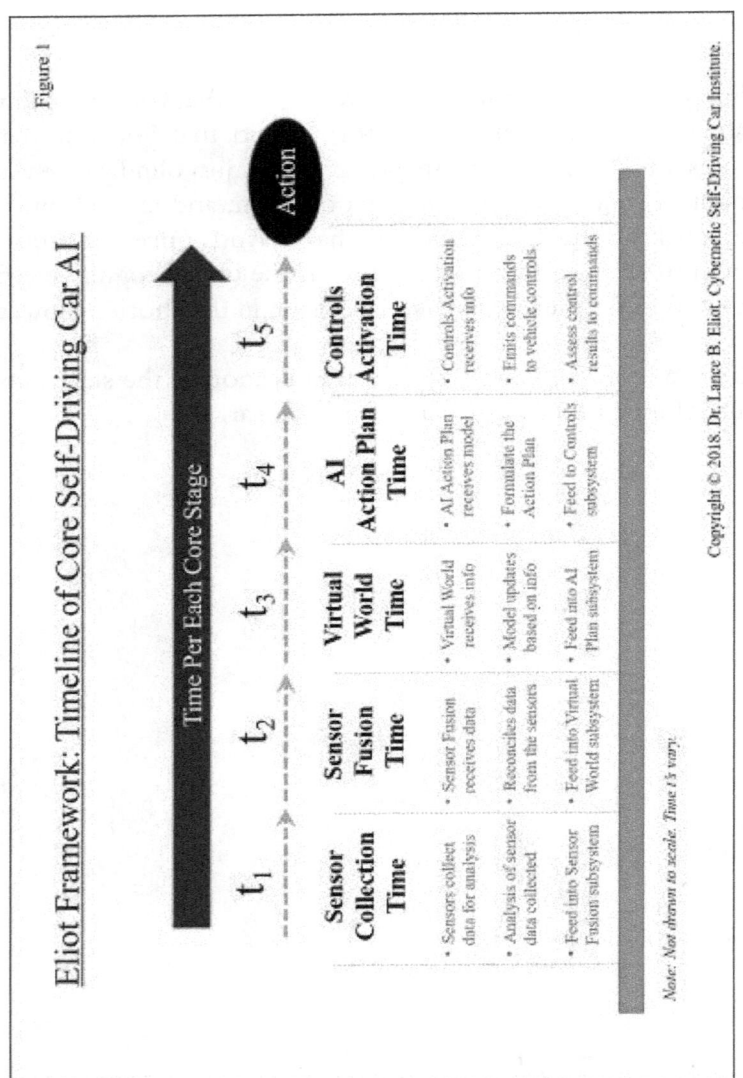

Figure 1

Eliot Framework: Timeline of Core Self-Driving Car AI

Time Per Each Core Stage

t_1 — Sensor Collection Time
- Sensors collect data for analysis
- Analysis of sensor data collected
- Feed into Sensor Fusion subsystem

t_2 — Sensor Fusion Time
- Sensor Fusion receives data
- Reconciles data from the sensors
- Feed into Virtual World subsystem

t_3 — Virtual World Time
- Virtual World receives info
- Model updates based on info
- Feed into AI Plan subsystem

t_4 — AI Action Plan Time
- AI Action Plan receives model
- Formulate the Action Plan
- Feed to Controls subsystem

t_5 — Controls Activation Time
- Controls Activation receives info
- Emits commands to vehicle controls
- Assess control results to commands

Action

Note: Not drawn to scale. Time t's vary.

Copyright © 2018. Dr. Lance B. Eliot. Cybernetic Self-Driving Car Institute.

The first stage involves getting sensor data and doing some rudimentary analysis of it, which we'll say takes an amount of time t1. The second stage is the sensor fusion that coalesces the sensor data and tries to resolve conflicts and bad data, and does so in an amount time t2. The third stage is the updating of the virtual world model, which is a representation of the self-driving car's surroundings and existing situation, and we'll say that this updating takes an amount of time t3. The fourth stage is the AI action plan that needs to be formulated, such as the different scenarios about how to avoid the pedestrian, and we'll say that this stage takes an amount of time t4. The fifth stage consists of issuing commands to the driving controls of the car, and we'll say this takes an amount of time t5. Note that t5 does not include the time for the car to react to the commands and take actions, it is only the amount of time needed to issue the commands to the driving controls and for those controls to receive the commands.

Thus, overall, we need an amount of total time consisting of Total Time = t1 + t2 + t3 + t4 + t5 in order to have the AI figure out what to do.

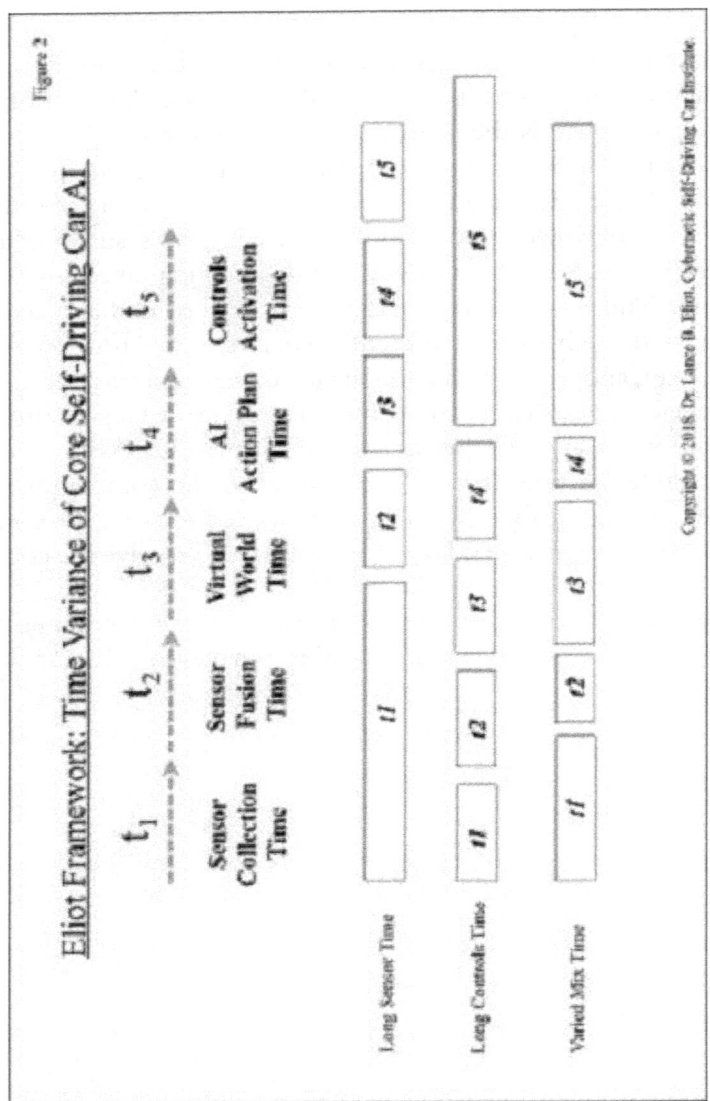

Figure 2

Eliot Framework: Time Variance of Core Self-Driving Car AI

As shown in Figure 2, these times of t1, t2, t3, t4, t5, will vary from moment to moment, and each will take its own amount of time. I say this to clarify that it is not as though we have predetermined that they are all the same amount of time, such as if we said that each would be a half second in length. Nor are these each the same amount of time, in the sense that t1 could be longer than or short than say t2, in any given circumstance. Also, keep in mind that these five stages are repeatedly looping, over and over, while the self-driving car is underway.

We might have an instance wherein the t1 is the longest of the times of the t2, t3, t4, t5 (see the first example shown in Figure 2). This would be an occasion of a long sensor time aspect. Generally, getting the sensor data is going to be one of the longest of the timings, since it involves collecting physical data and having to get it through the sensory devices and then into the processing of the AI system. Or, we might have a long time needed to issue commands (second example in Figure 2).

Overall, the amount of time will be mixed and varies (see the third example in Figure 2).

You might be wondering whether there is anything doing time tracking. The answer is yes, there is an element of the AI system that needs to be the Time Master.

Take a look at Figure 3.

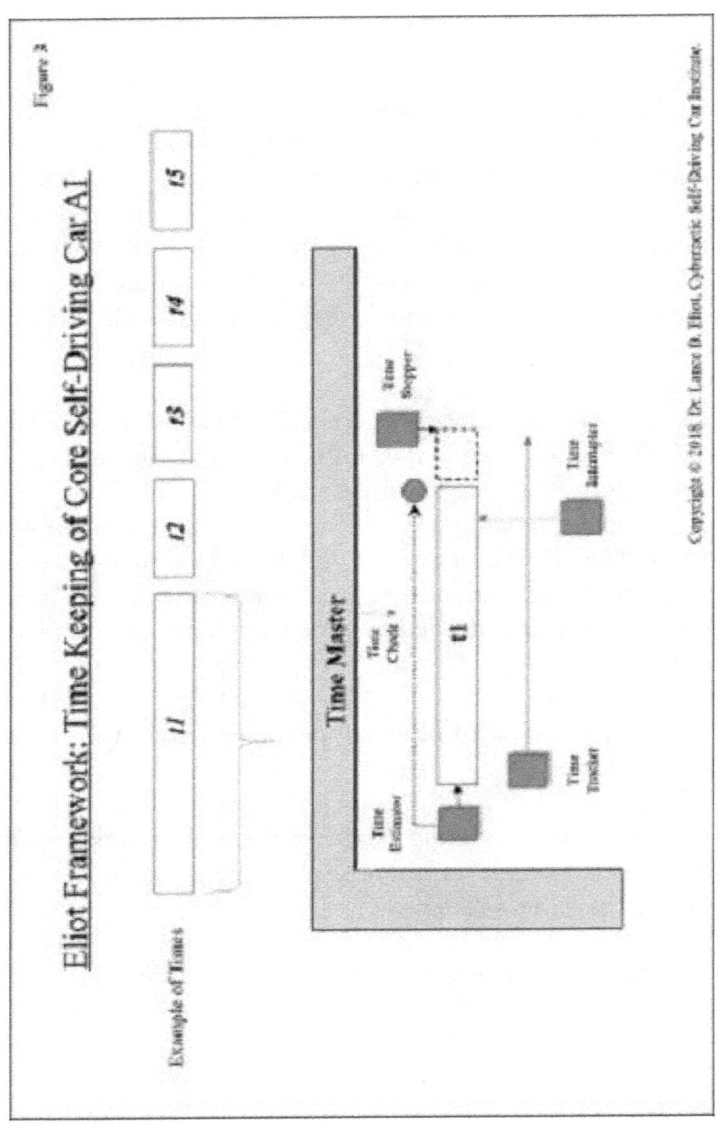

Figure 3

Eliot Framework: Time Keeping of Core Self-Driving Car AI

Copyright © 2018 Dr. Lance B. Eliot, Cybernetic Self-Driving Car Institute.

I've shown that we'll have for each of the t1, t2, t3, t4, t5 stages there is a system element that is keeping track of time. The t1 is shown as an example.

Before entering into any of the stages, a Time Estimator module is used to estimate how much time that the stage will take. This is crucial for purposes of being able to then figure out the total estimated time for all five of the stages, as will be further discussed in a moment.

There is a Time Tracker module that ticks time during the stage and is reporting how much time is being consumed. During the stage, a Time Check might be undertaken to gauge how well the stage is proceeding and ascertain whether it is going to finish on-time of the estimate, or go long or maybe go shorter. There is a Time Interrupter module that can choose to intercede during the stage, depending upon whether something else is occurring that needs to either momentarily disrupt the stage or divert the stage to achieve some other task. The Time Stopper module will aim to prevent a stage from going excessively long, which could happen for a variety of reasons, including that the stage might have gotten itself into some kind of loop that it can't get out of on its own.

Take a look at Figure 4 to see a situation whereby the estimation total time has been calculated as Q, and the allowable time is considered time R. In this case $Q > R$, which is bad because it means that the cognitive effort is going to take longer than the system wants it to take. This could be the circumstance of having 2 seconds to decide what to do about a pedestrian, but the initial estimate of the time required to decide about the pedestrian is say 4 seconds. In that instance, $Q = 4$, while $R = 2$, and so we have a problem that $Q > R$, or $4 > 2$.

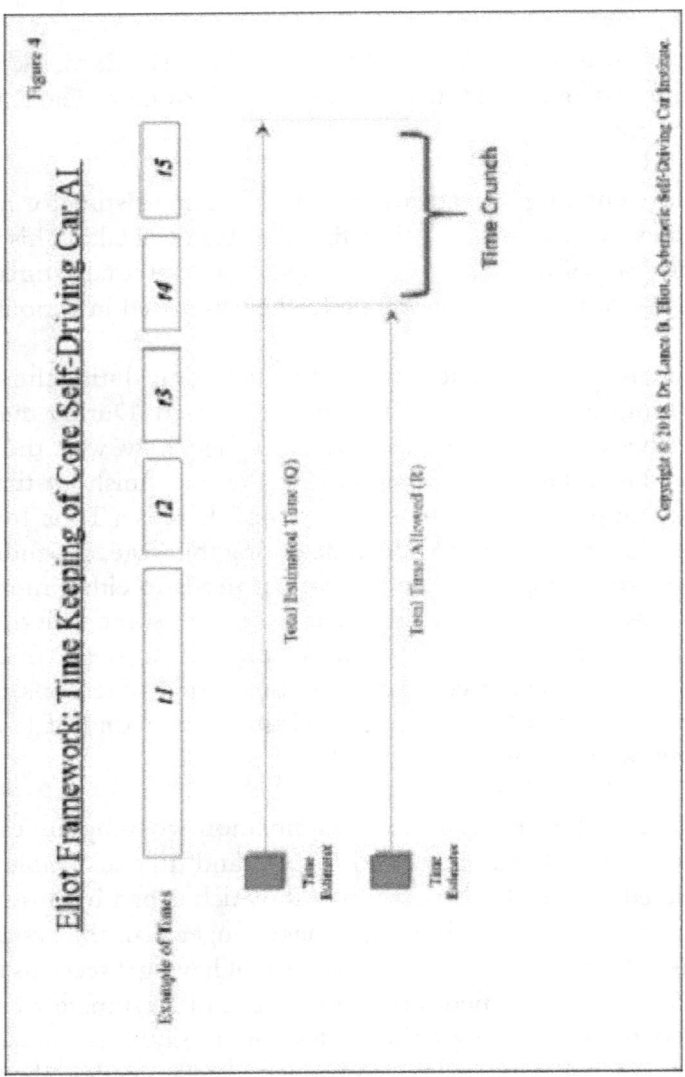

Eliot Framework: Time Keeping of Core Self-Driving Car AI

Figure 4

How would the system deal with such a time crunch?

Let's consider some scenarios.

Suppose a self-driving car is driving in downtown Los Angeles. The day of the week and the time of the day makes a big difference as to what is happening around the car. If it's a Sunday morning at 6 a.m., the odds are that the streets are empty, there's very little traffic, there are almost no pedestrians, there aren't likely bike riders, etc. In this case, the amount of sensory data that needs to be closely examined is relatively small, since there's few objects being detected and little movement surrounding the car. The virtual world model is relatively simple and barren. Any AI action plan is rather straight forward. The AI can quickly do the t1, t2, t3, t4, t5, over and over, and be moving the self-driving car along its way in the streets of downtown.

Let's instead consider a Monday early evening of around 6 p.m. in downtown Los Angeles. Cars have flooded into the streets and they are jockeying for position. Bike riders are everywhere, weaving into and out of traffic. Pedestrians are everywhere, including jaywalking and cutting into traffic. It's chaos. It's a mess. For this circumstance, the sensors are finding tons of objects that need to be assessed. The virtual world model is jammed with all sorts of indications. The AI action plan is complicated by all of this surrounding activity and potential threats. The t1, t2, t3, t4, t5 is going to stretch out.

What can be done to deal with the downtown driving scenario to allow for cognitive economy, if the AI and the self-driving car is having troubles trying to process all of the hectic activity in real-time and ensure that the self-driving car remains safely on the road?

One aspect is the bubble effect. You could have the AI opt to ignore anything that is beyond a close-in bubble of the self-driving car. Anything beyond five feet the AI decides that for the moment it will pretty much only consider if it somehow seems to be moving fast and toward the self-driving car. Otherwise, it just ignores it for the moment. This would be like a novice teenage driver that is overwhelmed when driving in downtown Los Angeles, and so they simply consider that their focus will be to continue driving forward, and they hope that everyone else will get out of their way.

This has risks associated with it, for sure. If you were an occupant in the AI self-driving car, would you be aware that it has opted to reduce the cognitive load and therefore is now possibly taking on greater risks of hitting something or getting hit? Most of us wouldn't know, and the AI self-driving car isn't being programmed to tell us. Some say that the AI self-driving cars have a duty to inform the occupants. Others say that when you do a ridesharing and have a human driver, the human driver is not under any obligation to tell you that they are taking mental shortcuts while driving the car.

Another cognitive shortcut for the AI could be to lump together objects.

For example, suppose there are eight pedestrians standing at the street corner up ahead. You could either try to track each one separately, or you might consider them as a clump of pedestrians. Cognitively dealing with the clump will save on cognitive cycles and you can trim the time it takes to figure out what's going on with those pesky pedestrians. This might work out OK, though if a specific pedestrian, let's say a small child, suddenly darts into the street, the question is whether the AI could have predicted this, and whether it therefore might have ensured that the self-driving car would avoid the child. If instead the pedestrians are being treated as a clump, it could be that the AI was not able to predict the chances of the behavior of a member of the clump.

Another cognitive shortcut involves templating a scene or situation. If the self-driving car has driven along this busy street many times before, it could already have prepared a model of the street and all of the likely aspects involved. For me, since I've driven in downtown Los Angeles for many years, I can predict when cars will pull out of a parking garage "unexpectedly" and be ready for it. I can anticipate that those cars in the right turn lane will realize they didn't intend to be in that lane, and they will at the last moment dart into the next lane to the left. These are all predictable based on having been in the driving scene before. I am able to reduce my own cognitive cycles since these aspects are all known beforehand and I am ready to have them happen.

Another aspect of the cognitive load involves the dynamics of motion. When the self-driving car is in motion, it is having to re-calibrate in real-time where it is, and where things around it are. It also should be predicting where other nearby in-motion objects will soon be. Experienced drivers anticipate that a car coming along on a cross-street will in say 2 seconds be potentially intersecting with them, and so must constantly be predicting the paths of other moving objects.

The AI is not only updating the virtual world model, but also using it for prediction purposes. It's almost like being an air traffic controller that is looking at planes and figuring out when they might intersect with each other. A particular plane is moving north to south at such-and-such speed, and in four seconds will be over here. Another plane is moving west to east, and will possibly intersect with the first plane at four seconds from now. These kinds of considerations need to be undertaken for the moving objects that are surrounding the AI self-driving car, involving moving cars, moving pedestrians, moving bicyclists, and so on, and of course the moving of the self-driving car itself.

Machine learning is involved in these activities too. Often using an artificial neural network, the AI is able to spot patterns in the nature of the traffic situations, and has a prior set of already identified patterns to make use of. One timing aspect that needs to be considered is how fast the neural network can generate a result for the AI to make use of. Suppose there's a neural network being used in the sensor fusion portion t2, and the neural network is going to take N amount of time to figure out the pattern. Imagine that we need to crunch down on the N amount of time because the self-driving car is in a tight predicament.

What we do is exercise beforehand our neural networks to get a gauge of how long they will take and thus we generally know what their likely timing will be in various circumstances. If you are sufficiently prepared beforehand, you can be ready to have the neural network take shortcuts, such as not make use of the entire network or otherwise take a faster approach to the pattern matching. Once again, this does likely raise risks, and so the short cutting of the neural network must be done in a prudent manner. As an aside, if the neural network is doing learning on-the-fly, you can gain some time by temporarily disabling that aspect until the time crunch efforts have subsided.

As they say, time flies.

They also say, don't waste time.

The AI of a self-driving car has to do a continual battle with time. The processors on-board the self-driving car can only go so fast. You can tweak the speeds by putting in faster processors and faster memory. That though does not obviate the need for the AI system to be aware of time and be watching time. This is a real-time system that involves life-and-death. Knowing how much time you have, and knowing how to get things done in time, are essential for achieving a successful AI self-driving car.

CHAPTER 5

SPEED LIMITS
AND
SELF-DRIVING CARS

CHAPTER 5

SPEED LIMITS AND
SELF-DRIVING CARS

I feel the need, the need for speed.

But, then again, some say that speed kills.

We have speed limits on our roadways, and I am sure there've been some days when you wished that there wasn't any limit at all, so that you could get to that baseball game on-time or get home sooner after work. Other days you probably see some crazy drivers that seem to be speeding recklessly and you wish that there was a laser gun that would automatically zap those cars and prevent them from being dangerous scofflaws. Speed limits, love them and hate them, we seem to be conflicted anyway you look at it.

There are advocacy groups that say our existing speed limits are too high. They argue that we need to bring down the speed limits to slower and more "reasonable" speeds. On the other side of this coin, there are advocacy groups that say we need to raise the speed limits. Indeed, some of those advocating faster speeds are even prone to saying that we should not have any maximum speed limit at all. In a kind of capitalistic viewpoint, they argue that it should be a "free market" and allow anyone to drive as fast as they want. Having restrictions on our driving speed is akin to restricting our freedom of speech.

In the early days of the automobile, the UK is famous for having enacted one of the first laws to regulate driving speeds, doing so in 1832 in response to "furious driving" by some early adopters of these new horseless carriages. Supposedly, the first person actually convicted of the crime of speeding occurred in 1896 and the driver was going an outrageously dangerous 8 miles per hour. Of course, as cars modernized, and as they became widespread, there gradually was a progressively increasing speed limit established. It kept going up, until the advent of the oil crisis led to a backlash against gas guzzling cars that seemed to consume too much gas after they exceeded a speed of around 55 miles per hour.

Nowadays, there are those that argue that the gas consumption curves of years ago are no longer applicable to the fuel efficiencies of modern day gas powered cars. They say that the fuel efficiency once used to set speed limits is woefully outdated. Furthermore, we are seeing more cars becoming electrically powered and the question is raised as to whether the gas fuel charts make any sense when our cars are powered instead by electricity. Those that concede the battery powered cars will change things are though quick to point out that there's at best 1% of all cars in the US that are electrically powered, and so they say come back and talk with them about speed limits when the other 99% of the gasoline gulping cars on the roadway become electrical.

The argument about fuel efficiencies is just one of the factors that goes into ascertaining speed limits. Yes, it is perhaps one of the most discussed topics and the 600-pound gorilla in the debate room, but there are other factors that get onto the table too.

Here's some factors that are used as arguing for setting speed limits:

- Can reduce roadway casualties due to car accidents and collisions that happen when going fast

- Can lessen the physical impact to our roadways that makes the roads spotty and full of potholes

- Can improve our air quality by reducing the amount of exhaust pollutants that occur when going fast

- Can make our roadways safer for non-car traffic such as bicyclists and pedestrians

- And can presumably be more fuel efficient (had to list it)

Each of those factors are readily open to discussion and debate. For example, advances in cars have dramatically lessened the amount of pollutants generated and some assert that there's a marginal indication that faster speeds also produce any significantly larger amount of air pollutants. In terms of roadways getting chopped up by going fast, some would say that with the improvements in tires and if the roads were paved the right way to begin with, there's little evidence that going faster is going to disproportionately tear up our roads.

For those of you that crave speed, you've likely gone to Germany to drive on the autobahns. There are many stretches of the autobahn that have no designated speed limit, or that offer an "advisory" speed limit but that you can choose to ignore if you wish. I remember when I lived in Frankfurt that I was astonished to be able to drive nearly as fast as I had the guts to push down on the accelerator pedal, and it made many of my long-distance driving trips on the autobahn both exciting and also terrifying. Unless you've been driving NASCAR race cars for a living, finding yourself driving at extremely high speeds is not for the faint of heart. I found that when I exited the autobahn, I was often bathed in sweat and my hands had been gripping the steering wheel in a near-death-like manner.

Like most states in the United States, California has a so-called "basic speed law" that refers to the notion that you are supposed to drive as a "reasonable man" would drive (the word "man" here is meant to indicate mankind, as in both men and women). You are not supposed to drive faster than is safe for whatever the current roadway conditions are.

Why My Friend Got a Speeding Ticket for Going 55 mph

I mention this because a good friend got a speeding ticket for driving 55 miles per hour on Pacific Coast Highway (PCH), which had a posted speed limit of 55 mph, and he was really upset. I asked him why a Highway Patrol officer would give him a ticket for doing the speed limit, and at first my friend said that they were just out to get him. Upon further inquiry, my friend eventually revealed that the stretch of the PCH had heavy fog at the time he was driving it, and it was soaking wet and partially flooded from recent rains. The officer told him that he was driving at an unsafe speed for the traffic conditions.

In short, the speed limit signs are intended for ideal driving conditions. Of course, the reality is that many people seem to think that these signs are merely advisory, and so they go much faster than what the signs say. One driver that I know well has told me several times that she perceives the speed limit signs as the minimum speed you should drive (this is a combination of humor and a bit of reality for her too). Some drivers see the speed limit signs as a kind of game – how much faster can they go, without getting caught. They are proud to report that they went 55 mph in a 25 mph zone and then challenge their friends to see if they can top it.

It's a matter of physics that the faster you go, the longer it's going to take to come to a halt. The stopping distances get larger at higher speeds. This is an important point because drivers tend to not take into consideration that as they reach higher speeds they are reducing their chances of stopping on a dime. Whatever they thought they could do at lower speeds is not the same at the higher speeds. Human drivers are notorious for misjudging stopping distances. They don't automatically recalibrate in their minds the nature of the higher speeds and the amount of true stopping distance they will need.

Since mankind can be kind of irrational about their driving speeds, mankind has equally come up with ways to try and make those irrational drivers become more rational. Besides the threat of getting a speeding ticket, there are additional methods of putting a rein on speeders. Traffic calming is one such technique. This refers to putting in place roadway obstacles or shaping the roads to try and prevent or at least mitigate the chances of speeding.

I'm sure you've driven in an area that has speed bumps on the roadway. Perhaps you've seen them near a school ground or in a parking lot. These physical humps are there to shake the teeth of the speeding driver and get them to slow down. It can be quite jarring to try and speed over a speed bump. When I see some nut trying to do so, I wait and watch, hopeful that I'll see their transmission drop out of the bottom of their car or maybe see the entire underbelly of the car become wrecked and disable the car for further movement. That's just my dream.

Another approach to traffic calming involves designing the roadway for slowing down traffic. Sometimes a street will be narrowed to force the flow of traffic into a single lane, which then ultimately slows down the overall traffic on that roadway. There was an effort here in SoCal to slow down a highly trafficked area by putting in an expanded bike lane. This seemed to be a good idea. It would make more space for bicyclists and encourage non-car options of transportation, and it would make the prevailing traffic move at a slower and safer pace.

One area that tried this had a pretty vigorously negative reaction by drivers. Their daily commute to work doubled or tripled. Also, cars opted to avoid the congestion on the main road and began to flood into the nearby neighborhoods, causing danger to children. Some contended that this was causing their property values to plummet. Local merchants said that their business was dropping because word spread that it was impossible to drive to their businesses to go shopping. The area was also a tourist spot, and tourism dried up, which then also caused businesses to lose more business. And so on.

Another solution involves using speed limiters on cars. You've likely not seen this. A speed limiter is either a device or software that will prevent a car from going above a certain speed. The simplest versions of a speed limiter are only focused on a maximum speed limit. It might for example be set to 70 miles per hour, and thus even if your car can go faster, the device won't let your car do so. It essentially bypasses your pressing on the accelerator pedal. With modern cars, you don't necessarily need a physical device to do this, and instead the software that regulates the acceleration of the car can be set with a limit.

More complex versions of the speed limiter allow for a multitude of settings. For example, there might be a setting that establishes a maximum speed for the car during daylight, and a different speed limit for nighttime driving. Currently, those limiters are relatively crude and can't do much in terms of being sophisticated about setting the speed limits. Also, it usually requires that you take your car into a dealership or someplace where they can put in place the limiter. The consumer has only a limited ability to tinker with the speed limiter.

I've seen some parents that did this on their cars for their children. The logic was that the teenage driver would be safer if they didn't drive more than the allowed speed limit. Some parents even insist that their teenage driver put an app on their smartphone that will keep track of movement, such that the app will know when the teenager is going more than walking speed. The app then reports to the parent as to how fast the teenager was going, including not only when driving a car but also when being an occupant in someone else's car (got to curtail those joy riding with friend's experiences!). As you can imagine, the teenagers aren't thrilled about this form of Big Brother tracking.

One of the criticisms of the speed limiters is that it might cause a restriction when you want to overcome the restriction. Suppose that you are driving your car and it has a speed limiter set to 55 mph. A rock flies off an overpass and smashes through the windshield and strikes your front seat passenger. You decide that you need to rush to the hospital to save the passenger. But, the limiter prevents you from doing so. Bad news! By the way, this actually happened recently that a rock flew through a windshield, hitting the husband while his wife was driving the car. She had the presence of mind to drive him to a hospital. I realize that you might say that this is an unfair rare example and that by-and-large there would be few valid exceptions to the speed limiter – yes, that's fine, but I can also say that when you need the exception, and even if rare, it could be a life killer.

One very rational criticism about going fast is that it really doesn't save you much time. For example, it has been pointed out that if you went at a speed of 80 mph for a 50-mile trip, and did so rather than going 75 mph, you would only save about 2 ½ minutes for the overall trip. Indeed, I've seen cars pass me on the main freeway between Los

Angeles and San Francisco that were going at least 90 mph, and yet I often catch-up with them at a roadside gas station, and they are lazily getting gas and stocking up on provisions at the mini-mart. The time they spent at this stop would readily use up any time they had "saved" by speeding far beyond the speed limit. It's not as though they were doing a race car type of pit stop with strict timing to get back right away onto the road. Their having sped seems senseless.

This few minutes' difference though could be a significance difference when driving even short distances, depending upon an emergency situation. For the wife that was driving her husband to the hospital, speeding could make the difference of his getting to the hospital in time to be saved. A counter-argument is that the panic driving of the wife and her speeding could actually cause other car accidents and maybe harm or injure others, while in her quest to have her husband saved.

In some areas of the country, the speed limit is established by first measuring the prevalent speed based on 85% of the traffic that flows on the given road. Based on that number, the speed limit is set within about 5 miles per hour of that overall average. This assumes that the final tabulation does not exceed a federally mandated cap or other caps in that jurisdiction. For many, they like the idea that the speed limit should be set by how people actually drive in an area, rather than as determined by a governmental body that regulates the use of the roads.

AI Self-Driving Cars Need to be Savvy About Speed Limits

What does this have to do with AI self-driving cars?

At the Cybernetic Self-Driving Car Institute, we are developing AI systems for self-driving cars and this includes being savvy about speed limits.

Let's consider some of the ramifications about speed limits and self-driving cars.

Those that believe in a utopian world of all self-driving cars, which I claim won't happen for a very long time since we currently have 200+

million conventional cars in the US and those aren't going away overnight, but anyway once someday that we do have all self-driving cars that then we can do something about our speed limits. I say this because suppose we take the human out of the equation for why we set speed limits.

If you assume that the human won't be driving any cars on our roadways, we no longer need to be concerned about a human drunk driver. If we also assume that the AI will be able to drive the car as well as or even better than a human proper driver, we will presumably have many less car accidents. For those that falsely believe we will end-up with zero accidents, I point out that there will still be accidents involving cars that hit debris in the roadway, or that blow out a tire and veer into another lane, or that hit a pedestrian that steps onto the roadway unexpectedly, and so on. We aren't going to have zero fatalities, and I'd ask that people stop claiming that it will happen.

So, given the aforementioned caveats, in theory we could increase the speed limits since we no longer have the human frailties of driving.

What about the other factors that we had covered earlier?

It was suggested that higher speeds harm the roadways in terms of physical impacts to the roadway. There's nothing magical about self-driving cars that will overcome this. Now, as mentioned, cars are getting better in terms of their design and so generally a better designed car, conventional or self-driving, will nonetheless extract less of a toll on the physical roadways.

In terms of improving air quality, again a self-driving car doesn't really impact this aspect per se, and it's up to how the car is designed that will make a difference, conventional or self-driving. Same generally goes for the topic of fuel efficiency. The point being that even if a self-driving car is a better driver than a human, going at high speeds will still produce the same amount of pollutants and be as fuel inefficient as if a human driver was driving, and so we would need to decide how important those factors are (having taken off the table the human driver frailties).

This brings us to the factor that our roadways would be safer at lower speeds due to the greater chance of avoiding non-car traffic accidents such as with bicyclists and pedestrians. The question then is whether an AI self-driving car, if allowed to go at speeds faster than our existing speed limits, would it have a tendency to be able to avoid these non-car traffic accidents, doing so at a better rate than if it were a human driver?

You might say that the AI system would hopefully be less likely than humans to get into these non-car accidents. This is based on the assumption of human frailties, namely that humans are apt to be sleepy when driving and fail to see a pedestrian, or be drunk, or otherwise not be as "flawless" as a machine would be. But, we need to be careful in assuming that the AI and the sensors of the self-driving car are of necessity more astute than a human driver and their human senses and human mind. It's a science fiction type of assumption that the AI and the sensors will work flawlessly, all of the time, and in every way.

In fact, it is unlikely that the AI and the sensors will be perfect machines. The sensors will at times falter and be unable to detect pedestrians and bicyclists. The sensors can fail entirely and the AI is left with a myopic understanding of the surroundings. Some of you will say that the odds of the sensors faltering or failing are miniscule and that I am misleading you about their error rates. Well, keep in mind that if we assume that all 200 million cars in the US alone are replaced ultimately with self-driving cars, and all of those self-driving cars have some X number of sensors, perhaps two dozen or more, and that those will fail or falter on some kind of probability basis, you are now looking at something that will happen in the large rather than in the small

Does it make sense to increase the speed limit in a world of self-driving cars?

We are going to have a mixture of human driven cars and self-driving cars for many decades, and so if we do increase the speed limit it would imply that human drivers could go faster too. In that case, we're back to the frailties of human drivers and what happens when they are allowed to drive faster. Some say that we could devote lanes to self-driving cars, and separate the human drivers from the self-driving cars. Imagine if you are driving on the freeway, and the HOV lane is reserved for self-driving cars. And, suppose further that those self-driving cars are allowed to go at a speed of 100 mph, or maybe at whatever speed they can go.

This could be a dangerous situation. Human drivers might veer into this special lane and cause a wreck. When self-driving cars try to get into the lane, it will be hard for them to reach the prevailing speeds in that lane as when coming from the conventional speed lanes. When self-driving cars exit from this special lane, they will be going at a much higher speed than the rest of the traffic. Overall, it could be a disastrous approach. Some might say that we just need to block off the special lanes and not allow any mixing with the human driven cars. Yes, this would help the circumstance, but it also would require a rather costly change to our roadway infrastructure, which maybe makes economic sense or maybe not.

I realize that an all self-driving car situation would allow for the self-driving cars to coordinate their efforts. Using V2V (vehicle-to-vehicle communications), the self-driving cars could let each other know when a self-driving car wants to get into a lane or exit from a lane. The other nearby self-driving cars would then be aware to allow for this movement of the other self-driving car. In that manner, it could be that we would not have any speed limit at all. The AI's of the self-driving cars would just agree to whatever speed seems to make sense for the prevailing situation.

This brings up too that the AI of the self-driving car can be a kind of speed limiter. The AI is going to decide what speed to go. Should it be programmed to never go faster than a set speed limit?

You could contend that AI self-driving cars will always be law abiding. They will always obey the speed limit. Assuming that the AI is indeed programmed for this, and that it works flawlessly in doing so, we are back to our earlier question about whether the speed limit should always apply or not, such as the case of the wife driving her husband to the hospital. If you were in a self-driving car, and your husband was bleeding and dying, and if the AI refused to go faster than the posted speed limit, would you be upset that the AI won't do your bidding and go faster?

If the AI is really sharp, it might be able to dialogue with the occupants and figure out that an emergency is taking place. Perhaps, in that case, the AI would have been pre-programmed that it can go as fast as it can achieve. This kind of notion though is a bit far-fetched and we'd likely need to still have some means of validating that the AI is doing the right thing, maybe an after-the-fact kind of verification. This also brings up whether all self-driving cars will be doing this in the same manner. If we have one auto maker make their self-driving car AI do one thing, and another do something else, in terms of speed limits, we're bound to have quite a mess.

Perhaps we should have a governmental regulation that indicates how the self-driving cars and their AI is to behave with regard to speed limits. Some would argue to keep the government out of such things, and instead maybe there should be an industry-based association that can set standards for this type of aspect. Others might say that the marketplace should decide, and leave it to each auto maker to provide whatever they believe the market most wants.

Speed limits can presumably become digitally-based in the future. We could still have posted speed limit signs, but they would be a digital display rather than a painted sign. This would allow for the speed limit to be changed at any time, as based on the time of day, the prevailing traffic conditions and so on. For an AI self-driving car, it could "read" the digital sign by using a camera sensor that's on the self-driving car. Or, the digital sign could emit a signal that transmits the posted speed limit.

If we did have all self-driving cars, we could do away with the speed limit signs altogether. In theory, the speed limit could be a virtual speed limit and the use of V2I (vehicle-to-infrastructure) system would communicate the speed limit to the self-driving cars. As self-driving cars drive down a particular street, the V2I lets them know that since it a road next to a school and since it is morning time when the kids are arriving, the speed limit is 5 mph. Once the kids are in the classrooms, the V2I communicates to any passing self-driving cars that the speed limit has been raised to 15 mph. And so on.

We might allow for AI self-driving cars to exceed the speed limit when there's an emergency, and maybe even when there isn't an emergency. Suppose we as a society decide that you can go faster than the speed limit, but you need to pay to do so. It's almost like a toll. Rather than paying a speeding ticket after you've speeded, this would be a pre-payment so that you could speed. Your AI self-driving car might use the V2I to make a request to exceed the speed limit, the V2I system decides the request is valid, charges on-line to the self-driving car owner, and then grants permission to the AI of the self-driving car to go ahead and speed. This though could also be perceived as elitist and allow the wealthy to readily speed while the poor would be relegated to the slow zone for AI self-driving cars.

Would we still need any traffic-calming capabilities in an all self-driving car world? This depends upon whether the self-driving car are able to communicate with the V2I. If there isn't an appropriate V2I, we might still need the speed bumps since otherwise the AI won't know that it should necessarily be going slowly in a parking lot. In terms of speed limiters, imagine that if we as a society wanted to suddenly make the entire country be a 35 mph maximum speed limit, in theory something could be broadcast to all AI self-driving cars that essentially instantaneously set the speed limit to 35.

This though assumes that all self-driving cars will be able to communicate with some kind of overarching governing system. We don't have that as yet. Will we want this? Some would say it makes sense to have an ability to access all self-driving cars at once, while others would say this bodes for dangerous times, such as if a hacker was able to suddenly make all self-driving cars throughout the country come to a halt (such as setting a speed limit of zero), doing so all at once.

Now that you've had a chance to think about the nature of speed limits, it hopefully has raised your overall awareness that it is not such an easy answer as to whether with AI self-driving cars we should have higher speed limits, or possibly even no speed limits at all. I would also urge you to realize that the day when we have all self-driving cars and no human driven cars is a long, long, long ways in the future. As such, whatever we want to do about speed limits, it will need to be undertaken in a world consisting of both human drivers and AI self-driving cars.

Maybe we'd have AI that when stopped by a police officer and asked whether it saw the speed limit sign, the AI would respond by saying yes, but it doesn't believe everything it reads. Drum roll please and ba-dum-bum-ching.

CHAPTER 6

HUMAN BACK-UP DRIVERS AND SELF-DRIVING CARS

Lance B. Eliot

CHAPTER 6

HUMAN BACK-UP DRIVERS
AND SELF-DRIVING CARS

How would you like to work as a human back-up driver in a state-of-the-art AI self-driving car?

Sounds glamorous. You can impress your friends and colleagues by bragging about going around town in the future of automobiles. You are the future. In a sense, you feel like an astronaut that is taking us to new planets and to new horizons.

Or, there's another view.

You sit in a car all day long, waiting to see if you need to do anything. Most of the time, you essentially do nothing. You are a cog in the great AI machine. Machines are taking over, and you are helping this to happen. You are the enemy of humanity. In the parlance of Star Trek, you are a dunsel (this was a term used in the fictional Star Trek series and was a word used by the Federation to refer to someone that had no particular useful purpose).

What's the truth?

Pretty much the job is more towards the less glamorous side. Indeed, as I'll explain next, it's a thankless kind of job that has high stress, and to do it right you need to have nerves of steel, incredible patience, and be on your toes at all times. This is not for the faint of heart. It is often long stretches of monotonous boredom, punctuated by moments of pure terror and semi-panic.

Unfortunately, the manner in which some auto makers and tech firms are selecting and fielding their human back-up drivers is not of the utmost attention. This is unfortunate since the notion of the human back-up driver is that when the AI cannot handle a situation or when it falters, the human back-up driver takes over the controls.

Thus, this is a life-or-death kind of job.

If the human back-up driver or operator does not do their task at the right time, it could mean that the self-driving car will crash or otherwise get into dire trouble. This could harm or kill the human back-up driver, it could harm or kill any other human occupants, it could harm or kill humans in other nearby cars by colliding with them, it could harm or kill pedestrians, it could harm or kill bicyclists, and so on.

You might at first say that any Uber or Lyft driver could readily do this job. Not exactly. If you are a hired ridesharing driver, your job consists of driving a car. You know that all of the time you are behind the wheel, you are driving the car. Your attention is likely focused on the driving task. It's what we normally consider the act of driving.

In contrast, as a human back-up driver, you are behind the wheel, but you are not actively driving the car. You are supposed to be pretending that you are driving the car, in the sense that your attention is riveted to the road and the driving environment, and you are poised like a cat, ready to pounce and take over the controls. Let's pretend that you try doing this for one hour. During that hour, you aren't actively driving the car, but you know that any a moment's notice you might need to do so.

If you cared about this, you'd likely be exhausted at the end of the hour. It's like a deadly game of having knives being thrown at you. You watch them coming, you need to decide in a split second whether any will hit you, and you might need to suddenly jump into action to catch one before it does. You can't predict beforehand how many knives are going to be coming at you. It all happens in real-time. They are endlessly coming at you. One after another, after another, etc.

Suppose that you did this for one hour, and then I asked you to do it for say eight hours at a stretch. And, I asked you to do this for five days a week. And I asked you to do this week after week.

What would happen?

For some, the stress would be overwhelming and they'd likely have a difficult time continuing with this job.

For others, they might actually like being on-the-edge and maybe become proficient.

For many, it becomes a job that you eventually start to let your guard down. Suppose that rather than a continuous stream of knives coming at you, instead I tossed one at you from time-to-time, but completely unpredictable times. The odds are that you'd become complacent. You would know that most of the time you wouldn't need to dodge or catch the knives. It would only happen on occasion, and so you would naturally begin to be less attentive to the task at hand.

Suppose further that I sometimes threw a knife at you, but other times I threw a relatively harmless water balloon. The water balloon might smack you, it might sting a little bit when it hits you, and you'd get wet. Overall, though, you'd be OK. Now, what happens to your attention span? You don't know when something is coming at you, and in some cases it is scary and possibly a killer (the knife), while other times it's going to hurt just mildly (the water balloon).

If you are the human back-up driver, there are going to be cases whereby you take over the control of the self-driving car when it was heading to a near death situation, such as maybe veering over a cliff or ramming into another car. There might also though be situations where the self-driving car starts to go faster than the speed limit, and perhaps you are supposed to prevent it from violating the traffic laws, and so you need to take over in those circumstances too. These are like the knives versus the water balloons.

You might be interested to know that there's been lots of studies of rats and what happens to then under stressful situations. Experiments have done similar kinds of low stress and high stress tests of rats, doing so by randomly shocking them severely versus doing a puff of irritating air at them. As you might guess, the rats eventually become erratic in their responses since they can't well anticipate what is going to happen and how or when to react to it. Please know that I am not suggesting that human back-up drivers are akin to rats, and I am simply saying that behavior of even the simplest can become befuddled by these kinds of hit-and-miss high-stress situations.

At the Cybernetic Self-Driving Car Institute, we are developing ways to systematically aid the human back-up drivers in their driving efforts, along with providing guidelines as to how to best identify, select, hire, train, field, and keep engaged these crucial self-driving car operators.

Notice that I said that these human back-up operators are crucial. Here's why.

If we are going to have self-driving cars learning to drive while on our public roadways, we need to be comfortable that the risks of the self-driving car going awry are low enough that we are willing to have the self-driving cars mixing with society. You can think of this like having novice teenage drivers on the roadways, but even less so in terms of proficiency and awareness. Though the teenager might have emotion that inadvertently causes them to make a wrong move, the emotionless AI software does not have the same smarts as a teenager and so can make mistakes in plenty of other ways.

Usually with a beginning novice teenage driver, there will be an adult in the car with them (a normal requirement for most states). The adult is supposed to be ready to take over the controls of the car. This is in any practical sense unlikely as the adult is seated beyond the actual controls of the car. Yes, the adult can reach over and try to do the controls, but in reality this is not very easy to do. In that sense, we generally accept that the adult is there more so to provide coaching to the student driver, rather than truly be there to immediately handle the controls when needed.

For the self-driving car, the human back-up driver is sitting directly at the driving controls, which is much better than when having the adult seated next to a student driver. The human back-up driver has unfettered access to drive the car. They can respond immediately as needed, assuming they are paying attention and alert to do so.

The human back-up operator is our last line of defense.

If the AI of the self-driving car falters or fails, it is the human back-up driver that is intended to prevent a calamity. Without the human back-up driver, we would all be at much higher risk of having unattended AI self-driving cars that could go wacky and there'd be no immediate way to stop it. As an aside, I know that some of you will bring up the topic of remote operators as an alternative to the in-the-car human back-up driver – please note I've previously covered in other of my writings the topic of remote operators and I won't repeat those aspects herein.

So, we definitely need the human back-up drivers for us to proceed with AI self-driving cars on our public roadways. Without the human back-up drivers, we either would need to accept a much higher risk of calamity, or we would need to decide that self-driving cars can only go on private roads until they are so well proven that they are permitted onto public roadways. There are some that believe we should be confining self-driving cars to private roads, but the counter-argument by the auto makers and the tech firms is that you'll either need years and years of this before we'd have self-driving cars perfected, or that you'd never be able to "perfect" a self-driving car at all without it's encountering the variety of situations faced on our public roadways.

Disengagements

One of the most dreaded words for human back-up drivers is the word "disengagement" since it means that a human operator had to take over the AI self-driving car.

You might think that the human back-up operator should be happy to count disengagements, because it presumably means that the human driver was able to prevent an AI self-driving car from doing something untoward. The operator did what they were supposed to do. They saved themselves and the rest of us from a calamity.

The bad news is that disengagements are considered a problem for the auto makers and tech firms because it is considered a black mark. In theory, if the AI self-driving car is working perfectly, there should never be any disengagements. Therefore, the goal is to have zero disengagements. Thus, if the human driver brings about a disengagement, it tacitly is a sign that the AI is not perfected. It means that there's something wrong with the AI self-driving car.

You might say that it is unfair to consider disengagements in this manner. For example, suppose that the AI self-driving car blew a tire, which has presumably nothing to do with the car being a self-driving car, and suppose the human driver took over. Well, the counter-argument is that the AI should have figured out how to deal with the blown tire. The AI is supposed to be able to do anything a human driver can do, therefore, there should never be a need for a human driver to take over. If the human driver takes over, it means that the AI wasn't as good as a human driver.

This produces added stress onto the shoulders of the human back-up driver. They know that if they do a disengagement, it generally means that something is amiss with the AI self-driving car, but the auto maker and tech firm don't want that to happen. On the other hand, if the human driver does not do a disengagement, and if the self-driving car slams into a wall, it's death and destruction as a result. Certainly the human back-up driver does not want that to happen.

Shouldn't the AI developers be enthusiast to have a disengagement in the sense that it possibly tells them that there's something in the AI that needs to be further developed or enhanced? Wouldn't they want to know? The whole point of the roadway testing is to find the bugs and imperfections, learn from them, fix and improve the AI, until the point at which it becomes a true self-driving car. The more clues provided, the sooner this can get accomplished.

Well, it's not that easy. Right now, many of the regulations require the auto makers and tech firms to publish the counts of disengagements. Sadly, the media has grabbed hold of these numbers and uses them to pound away at whether the auto maker or tech firm is getting closer or further away from having a true self-driving car. As such, it behooves the auto maker and tech firm to try and keep the number of disengagements as small as possible. Of course, they already presumably want a small as possible number of disengagements anyway, since it suggests that their self-driving car is getting closer to be ready to be a true self-driving car.

But, this also distorts possibly the nature of the testing. It's reminiscent of the public relations nightmares faced by companies that make rockets. When they do a rocket test, the media will howl to the rafters when the rockets go amiss or explode on the pad. This proves that the rocket is not ready for prime time, says the media. The stock price of the rocket company plummets. How are they supposed to be able to do genuine testing if they are going to get castigated each time that a test shows something useful to aid them toward perfecting the rocket?

You might then be tempted to only test rockets that you know will work perfectly, even if it means that you aren't readily making progress toward making a better rocket. This same logic can be applied for self-driving cars. It might be easier to just have your self-driving car be driven in situations that there's little chance of a disengagement. Have the self-driving car drive around a small town that has little variety in terms of pedestrians that dart into the street or wild human drivers, and so this will hopefully reduce the number of disengagements.

The media then when reporting disengagements would make it seem that one self-driving car is obviously better than another, simply due to the lesser number of disengagements. This can be misleading and foolish because we aren't comparing the number of disengagements per capita, such as per mile driven or some such metric. Even there, though, miles driven in a small town are not the same as miles driven in a big city with tight streets and tons of traffic.

One issue is that there's not a clear cut standardized definition that everyone is using for a disengagement. The simplest definition is that it involves the human taking over the control of the self-driving car. But, it does not provide for any kind of why they did so. Some states require the why, some do not. Some allow it to be any kind of open text, and so it is difficult to gauge what the reason really was and it is problematic to compare it to others that are also reporting disengagements.

We also would likely want to know what the circumstance was and the length of time of the disengagement. If the human driver took over for a split second, it presumably might mean that the AI was just needing a nudge, while if the human driver took over for 20 minutes it might mean that something more serious was afoot with the AI. But, this is also hard to compare, since some firms have a policy that once a disengagement occurs, the human driver is supposed to continue doing the driving and bring the self-driving car to a spot where the developers can inspect it or otherwise review the self-driving car.

Consider another important aspect about disengagements, namely, was the disengagement a valid one or an invalid one?

Suppose the human driver opts to do a disengagement, doing so because they perceived that an accident was about to occur. How do they prove this? The AI developers might say that there was nothing wrong with the AI and it could have handled the situation. The human driver insists that they felt that the AI wasn't slowing down or swerving, or whatever, and so they judged that it was time to take over. But, the AI team might insist that this was mistaken by the human and the human should have allowed the AI to see things through.

You tell me, who's right and who's wrong?

It is hard to be able to "prove" that something bad could have happened, and so the human driver is once again under great stress. They not only don't know when the moment will arise to take over, they might also be second guessed as to why they did the takeover. Furthermore, they will likely be considered as skittish if they do too many takeovers. The odds are that a high number of takeovers or disengagements could lead to them getting fired.

The auto maker or tech firm would likely say that someone with excessive disengagements is not a good back-up driver because they are needlessly stopping the AI from driving the car. Ideally, the human back-up driver should only be doing valid disengagements and not doing any invalid disengagements.

This is the formula that is at times used:

Optimal # of disengagements = Maximum (Valid disengagements) – Minimum (Invalid Disengagements)

In theory, we want the human back-up driver to always do a valid disengagement, presumably therefore saving the self-driving car from getting into a calamity, and we want to minimize the number of invalid disengagements, preferably being zero. We'd of course also like to have the maximum number of valid disengagements be zero, since this means that no disengagements were needed at all.

Take a look at Figure 1.

I show a disengagement curve that depicts over time the number of driving incidents and the frequency of disengagements. What should be happening is that at first the frequency is high, and gradually after those are fixed, the number beings to drop. At some point, there are fewer and fewer left. The remaining ones are often in some obscure aspects of the AI that rarely occur.

There is a stress line that rises from left to right. The stress at the start is not quite so high because the disengagements are occurring with high frequency and easy for the human driver to identify and undertake. Gradually, as the frequency drops, the stress rises due to the aspect that now the human driver does not know when the takeover will need to happen. As mentioned earlier, they enter into a point of not knowing when to be alert and when they can relax.

There are two zones, the first zone is the predictable repeats, zone

A. The second zone is the unpredictable intermittent instances. When a human driver gets into zone B, they are at a high stress level as they await that sudden moment at which they'll need to spring to action. It probably won't be something obvious. It will likely be a driving situation that's oddball and will occur seemingly out of left field.

At this juncture too, the AI developers are likely hoping that there won't be any disengagements. The perception is that things are coming along swimmingly. This adds pressure to the human driver. The human wants to avoid making an invalid disengagement, but not incur the injury or death that might happen if they avoid making a valid disengagement.

I've seen some crazy things like one company that tied their pay of the human drivers to the number of disengagements. Imagine that you know that you'll get paid more if you avoid doing a disengagement, and so now you'll figure that it's worth it to take those chances like running with the bulls in Pamplona in order to have a fatter paycheck (you calculate the odds of getting injured or killed in a different manner due to the pay aspects). Trying to tie pay to having a high number of disengagements is equally problematic because then the human driver will just keep doing disengagements right and left to get paid more.

There was one firm that provided a quota to the disengagements. During your 8-hour shift, we expect 2.5 disengagements, the human drivers were told. What do you do with that? Do you wait as long as possible during your shift, and then force the 2 or 3 disengagements if you've otherwise had none? A quota or threshold for this kind of work has little in the way of being practical.

Human Engineers

Some firms opt to have the human back-up driver be accompanied by a human engineer in the self-driving car. They usually sit in the backseat and will have some form of monitoring equipment to detect what the self-driving car is doing. This can be handy since the engineer can quickly assess when a disengagement occurred as to what the self-driving car was doing. The engineer might not be able to do a full diagnosis by themselves, but at least they'll have had direct exposure to whatever was going on with the self-driving car and the driving situation.

I say this because it can be hard after a self-driving car journey to recreate what happened when the human driver took over. Sure, you can inspect the camera footage and the radar data, and so on, but there's an element of having been there, being in the moment, which can add valuable insight that any second guesser sitting in an office or lab three days later is not going to have handy.

These engineers serve another purpose which is often unstated and unheralded. They can talk with the human driver and keep them company. This can be a big boost to the human back-up driver. It can spur the back-up driver to be more attentive and stay attune to the driving situation. Otherwise, things can get pretty lonely for the human back-up driver. The human back-up driver is more apt to let their minds wander when there isn't an engineer present.

You could counter-argue that maybe the engineer will distract the back-up human driver. Maybe it's better to allow the human back-up driver to be solitary and remain utterly focused on the driving task. I'd say that might make sense for very short periods of time, but when you are thinking about a 4 hour shift or an 8-hour shift, I'd tend to go with having that engineer in there.

Some auto makers or tech firms that view the engineer as only there for purposes of monitoring are tempted to say that they should get rid of those engineers from being in the self-driving car. Just be recording whatever happens and you can always play it back later on. Plus, the cost of having that engineer in the self-driving car just drives up your costs, seemingly needlessly. The problem there is that the viewpoint is based on only seeing the engineer as a monitoring tool, and not as a fellow human that can interact with the human back-up driver. You need to consider the full sense of benefits of having the engineer, and weigh that against the added cost, and so if you undervalue the benefits then it does mistakenly seem like the added cost is not worthwhile.

Attention of the Back-up Driver

Some say that the solution to ensuring the attention of the human back-up driver involves adding automation to keep track of the human driver and spark them to remain focused to the driving task. For example, the steering wheel can have a mechanism that keeps track of the driver's hands, and then alerting them to keep their hands on the steering wheel. Another is facial recognition to detect that their head is facing forward. Another is eye movement recognition to detect that their eyes are locked on the road ahead and not looking off to the side or downward.

These are certainly valuable ways to help keep the human driver glued to the driving of the self-driving car. We are seeing these same kinds of systems being placed into the Level 3 and Level 4 self-driving cars, for which the human driver is still responsible for the driving task, even if the automation is performing some aspects of the driving task.

Still, as mentioned before, it's hard to remain alert when you are not actually driving the car. Yes, you are seated in the driver's seat. Yes, your head is facing forward. Yes, your eyes are on the road. Yes, your hands are at the ready on the steering wheel (but not actually steering). Does this though provide sufficient engagement to ensure that the human back-up driver is ready to take over the self-driving car?

We also need to consider the Human Computer Interface (HCI) aspects of the human back-up driver and the AI of the self-driving car. Will the AI alert the human back-up driver when something is starting to go amiss, or is the back-up driver expected to figure this out on their own? If the AI does alert the human back-up driver, in what manner does it do so, such as via audio tone, flashing lights, or verbal messages? What is the time delay between trying to inform the back-up driver and them being able to comprehend what the AI is trying to tell them?

There is the possibility that the AI will try to convey one thing, such as there's a kid on a bike to the left of the car and so watch out, when maybe the real problem is that a huge truck is coming at the self-driving car from the right and will take out everyone and everything. The back-up driver won't know for sure that the AI knows what is really happening, and nor whether it is conveying something relevant to the back-up driver.

If the AI doesn't provide any kind of warnings to the back-up driver, this means that the back-up driver has no idea whether the AI is comfortable with the driving situation or not. The back-up operator needs to second guess the AI. Maybe the AI knows what to do. Maybe the AI has no idea what to do. The back-up operator has no immediate means to ascertain those aspects.

We have been experimenting with the back-up operator carrying on a conversation with the AI of the self-driving car, similar to if the back-up driver was talking to a teenage novice driver, thus allowing the human driver to find out what the AI is doing, and also further engages the human driver into the driving task.

There have also been suggestions of using gamification to engage the human driver. One approach involves having a Heads Up Display (HUD), and the human driver is watching it and kind of playing a game of being able to keep up with what it shows. This HUD is showing aspects of the roadway and so it directly pertains to the task at hand of keeping aware of what the situation of the self-driving car is.

These are ways to keep the human back-up driver physically engaged, such as their hands and their head posture, and ways to keep the human back-up driver cognitively engaged (keeping their mind on the driving situation).

For training purposes, some of the auto makers or tech firms do barely any training of their human back-up drivers. Pretty much, if you can breathe and can drive a car, they let them do this task. Others take this a bit more seriously and train them on what the self-driving car is doing, thus increasing the chances of making sounder decisions about disengagements. I tend toward wanting to try and get the human back-up driver to feel that they are indeed part of the solution toward achieving self-driving cars, rather than just a kind of bus driver that maybe will take the wheel but otherwise has no real importance to the matter. I'd say that motivation can be a big plus for having an engaged human back-up driver.

How safe are we?

If the auto makers and tech firms don't do a good job of identifying, selecting, training, fielding, and updating their human back-up drivers, they are pretty much putting us all at a heightened risk. There will be a false sense of being "risk free" simply because a human is sitting in the self-driving car and ready to drive. The reality is that these human back-up drivers are key to preventing calamities, which can make-or-break the advent of self-driving cars. Tossing anyone into this role, paying them minimum wage, and pretending that you have human back-up operators is both a sham and a shame.

It's not much of a glamorous job. We all will only hear about the human back-up operators when a self-driving car goes awry and the human driver did nothing or took the wrong action. The rest of the time, they are out-of-sight and out-of-mind. I'd implore the auto makers and tech firms to not treat this role as something insignificant. They are the back-up to your self-driving car, and to the future of self-driving cars, along with my safety and everyone else's safety while you are testing your AI self-driving cars on our public roadways. That's a big deal.

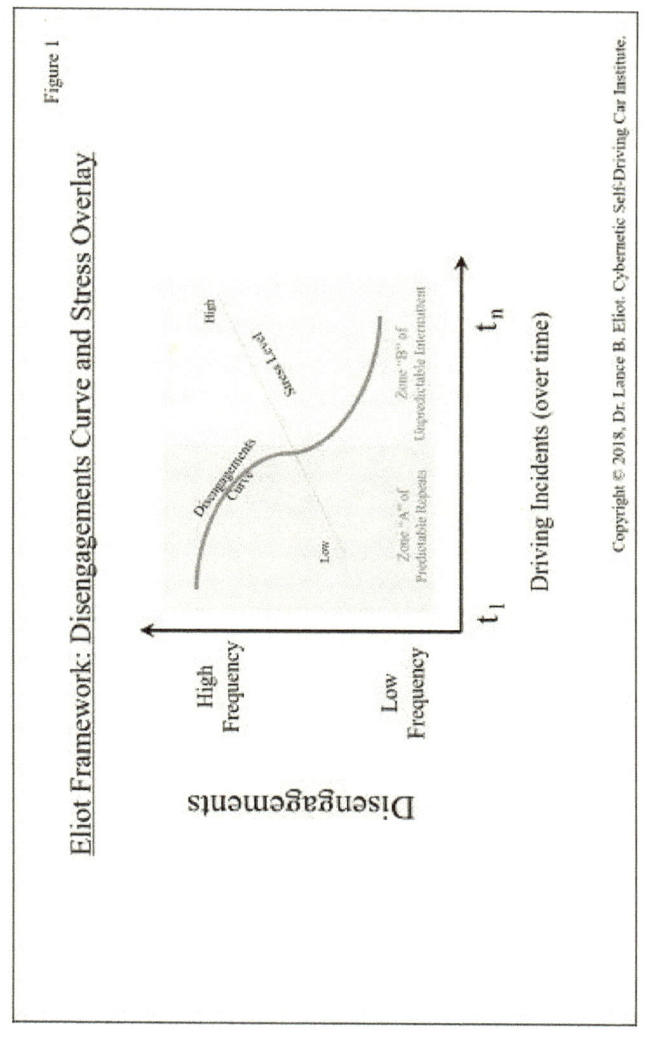

Figure 1

Eliot Framework: Disengagements Curve and Stress Overlay

Copyright © 2018, Dr. Lance B. Eliot, Cybernetic Self-Driving Car Institute.

CHAPTER 7
FORENSIC ANALYSIS
UBER SELF-DRIVING CARS

CHAPTER 7

FORENSIC ANALYSIS UBER
SELF-DRIVING CARS

I write a regular on-line column on AI and in my column published on April 27, 2017, I stated this:

"I expect that we will soon have a self-driving car crisis-in-faith because some self-driving car will plow into a pedestrian. It is bound to happen."

Sadly, prophetic.

You might be aware that in Tempe, Arizona on Sunday, March 18, 2018 in the evening around 10 p.m., an Uber self-driving car, containing a human back-up operator at the wheel, ran into and killed a female pedestrian, 49-year-old Elaine Herzberg, whom had entered into the street outside of a crosswalk and in the front of the oncoming self-driving car. Reportedly, the self-driving car was doing about 40 miles per hour when it hit the victim.

Besides the terrible tragedy of having killed the pedestrian, an especially alarming aspect is that reportedly the self-driving car took no evasive action whatsoever, and, furthermore, the human back-up operator also reportedly took no evasive action.

This comes as a shock to many.

Well, they need to prepare themselves for many more such shocks. I say this because some are currently assuming that if this is an issue with Uber's self-driving car that it is somehow confined only to Uber's self-driving car (a Volvo). Presumably, all that needs to happen is to discover what the technological problem was, make a quick fix to their self-driving cars, and the world just moves along. This is narrow thinking.

Though it is the case that each of the auto makers are generally taking their own development approaches to their self-driving cars, and therefore this potential problem might not exist in those other self-driving cars, and whatever might have been a problem in this instance will not necessarily be a problem with other self-driving cars, though it could be and it's worthwhile to consider the ramifications as such – meanwhile, you need to be mentally ready for the aspect that other self-driving cars are bound to have some other kinds of problems that could potentially lead to a similar result.

I will therefore update my prediction of last year:

"In spite of whatever is learned from this recent incident, we will soon have another self-driving car that plows into a pedestrian, which will then shake to its core the self-driving car industry and a massive crisis-in-faith will ensue."

We need to consider that this is not merely a technological problem, which is the simplest way to cast the incident. There is a moonshot race toward being the first to produce a self-driving car that has regrettably put safety at a lesser priority than it deserves, and for which once we have enough self-driving cars on our roadways that the risks of the safety factors will play out in front of the public view. It's like spinning a roulette wheel and eventually the number is going to come up.

Let's be clear, yes, this is a technological issue, but also along with being a societal issue, a business issue, an ethical issue, etc. Don't trivialize it but trying to make it seem like it is just some bug in code and once we find it that we're all done with this matter.

Here's some of the questions that have been trending in the media about this Uber incident:

- How could a self-driving car have hit a pedestrian (they are supposed to be programmed to not do so)?

- Aren't self-driving cars going to bring us "zero" fatalities, which is what has been promised for the advent of self-driving cars?

- Even if somehow the self-driving car did nothing, isn't the human back-up operator there to take over and prevent anything from happening (for which the self-driving car could not otherwise detect or prevent)?

- Etc.

If the above sends chills up your spine, here's something else to realize, namely that the latest version of self-driving cars are being built with no means to have any human occupant be able to directly handle the brakes, the steering wheel, and otherwise have no access to the driving controls of the car at all. In this case there was a human operator, so at least there was a chance that the human operator might have been able to avert the incident. True Level 5 self-driving cars, which are supposed to be able to drive without any human intervention, won't even have the chance per se of a human trying to take over control of the self-driving car.

Now, before I get clobbered by everyone in the self-driving car industry, I want to emphasize that I am a huge proponent of self-driving cars. My firm is even developing AI software for self-driving cars. What I find worrisome is whether we are giving enough attention to safety. The rush toward wanting to be the first to have self-driving cars, which is fueled by the media attention that goes with it, and the frenetic atmosphere of the auto makers and tech firms wanting get to the moon first, it has unfortunately also led to safety getting less attention than it deserves.

If the Uber self-driving car had detected the pedestrian and tried to take evasive action, we'd be having a different conversation right now. It would be about what it did and how much effort it took to try and avoid hitting the pedestrian. But, the aspect that it seemingly did nothing is the part that catches our breath.

Likewise, if the Uber self-driving car had at least alerted the human operator, or if at least the human operator had taken over the controls and tried to avoid the pedestrian, we'd be having a different conversation. But, the aspect that the human operator seemingly did nothing is the other part that catches our breath.

I'd like to address these questions and use the Uber incident as a basis for doing so.

At the Cybernetic Self-Driving Car Institute, besides developing AI self-driving car systems and being a keen observer of the marketplace, we also do audits of self-driving car software and designs and perform as forensic specialists or expert witnesses regarding self-driving cars.

This Uber incident is keenly of interest to us and everyone else in the self-driving car industry. It is widely hoped that the underlying technological elements will be revealed by Uber. Whether they will do so is an open question. No one wants to reveal their inner proprietary secrets. That's a given. We'll have to see in what manner and detail the matter is reported, and whether it is done so voluntarily or under pressure by legal or regulatory bodies. The incident is being investigated by the NTSB (National Transportation Safety Board) and the NTHSA (National Traffic Highway Safety Administration), which is important and helpful to the matter, but you should also be prepared for a lengthy time period before much is revealed about their findings.

I will provide herein a kind of armchair forensic analysis of the March 18, 2018 incident.

Keep in mind that as I write this, it has only been about a week since the incident occurred, and so as I write this I do so with almost no details about the accident. It will be weeks or months before much more is publicly known about the incident. For a while, whatever had been collected or analyzed will be under wraps. As such, I am going to provide an "armchair" forensic analysis, meaning that I can only offer some educated guesses and speculation about what maybe happened.

This speculation though is actually useful because it lays out the various scenarios of what might have occurred. It also will help those of you interested in AI self-driving cars to have some further introspective about what goes on inside self-driving cars.

I cannot reasonably reach any definitive conclusions about what happened, but I can at least shed light on what might have happened and what to be on the look for. It will be interesting later on to see if I was able to land on anything that actually turns out to be the true culprits or reasons for the accident, which hopefully we'll all know once the actual evidence is explored and the investigations are completed and published.

About Forensics

Forensics is a type of science that undertakes an investigation to provide helpful insights for both criminal and civil cases. Most people tend to think of forensics as only for criminal cases, and we see this aspect portrayed by actors in many TV shows and films, but the same kinds of forensic analyses are often needed in civil matters too. If two cars smack into each other, and there's no injuries and no significant damages, the matter could likely get mired in a civil case of one party suing the other for financial compensation. It is likely that forensics experts would be called upon to participate in assessing the circumstances and providing potential insights and even actual testimony for the case.

Sometimes a forensic specialist will go to the actual scene of an incident and collect evidence, while in other instances they will mainly work in a lab or office and perform their analysis and conduct needed research there. The techniques used by forensic specialists will vary depending upon the nature of the case. Also, there are at times controversy about the techniques used, in the sense that some techniques are considered open to question or interpretation, and so you can have one forensic specialist that claims one thing and another one that claims something completely different.

Indeed, the two sides of a case, such as for criminal cases the prosecution and the defense, will line up forensic experts that are likely to go head-to-head about their respective findings. This is an important point because the layperson often assumes that the forensics is cut-and-dry, black-and-white, and there isn't any ambiguity or room for debate. In matter of fact, the odds are that for any complex case you can end-up with seemingly diametrically opposed conclusions by two fully qualified forensics specialists, each of which uses a particular technique or approach, and has made certain assumptions based on whatever evidence has been gathered.

For car accidents, there usually isn't a civil lawsuit because the insurance companies that represent the drivers will duke it out as to which side should pay what. Most of the time, they work this out somewhat amicably (but fiercely). There are occasions though when an injured party believes that they aren't getting a fair shake, and so they proceed to file a civil lawsuit. Typically, the insurance companies will then represent the respective drivers for the case, but this depends upon various aspects of the case.

We all recognize that if you get caught driving drunk, or Driving Under the Influence (DUI), you are usually subject to criminal penalties and especially when involved in a car crash. If you've caused property damage and/or injuries, there can be some pretty severe penalties involved. What many don't realize is that you can also be charged with reckless driving, a criminal offense, even if you weren't DUI. Most states require that you drive your car in a sound manner, and so if you do not do so, it can be considered reckless driving. It won't matter that you were perfectly sober. Driving in a manner that causes damages or injuries is considered a violation of the law. Wet reckless is when you are DUI at the time, while dry reckless is when you were reckless and not intoxicated.

In the state of California, reckless driving is considered a misdemeanor as per California Vehicle Code Section 23103: "A person who drives in a vehicle upon a highway in willful or wanton disregard for the safety of persons or property is guilty of reckless driving." Conviction can lead to county jail time for up to 90 days plus potentially a fine of up to $1,000. If there are significant property damages or injuries, things can get much worse in terms of the charges leveled and the outcome for the guilty party.

Potential Charges

For the Uber incident, there could be criminal charges involved, and there could be civil lawsuits involved.

It is possible that criminal charges might be levied against Uber, if the formal investigation concludes there was some form of recklessness or other failing on the part of Uber to ensure that their AI and the self-driving car was operating properly and appropriately.

There could also be criminal charges levied against the Uber human back-up operator, if the investigation concludes that the human operator failed to perform their duty.

Even if there aren't any criminal charges, the odds of a civil lawsuit are probably high, though supposedly the women that was killed was homeless, and so the lawsuit would need to be undertaken by someone connected to her, which no one has yet come forward as such. We'll probably see a civil suit launched within the next 30-days, I'd guess.

Data About What Happened

There are various potential pieces of evidence that can be used to try and ascertain what happened. I'm sure that the on-scene investigation gathered the physical evidence at the scene of the incident. It would be important to see whether there were any tire marks to indicate whether the Uber car was braking or not, and to study the damage done to the self-driving car, and other damages. The various aspects of the surrounding environment are crucial too, including the roadway surface, the layout of the roadway, nearby objects, and so on.

There haven't been any human witnesses that have come forward as yet.

Meanwhile, two videos were released, one that was from the Uber self-driving car via a video camera that was pointed forward, and a second video that was pointed inward at the human back-up operator.

It's handy that the videos were released, but there's a lot more we'd all like to know, including this:

- Blackbox recorder in the Uber self-driving car

- Processor memory of the on-board systems

- Uber/Volvo over-the-air in-the-cloud system

If there's a blackbox recorder in that Volvo, presumably it could be inspected and the recording of the car status might tell whether the AI system was engaged. This determination is partially based on whether or not the blackbox survived intact (it should have since the damage to the car was relatively minimal), whether or not it is readable, and whether or not it was appropriately recording the car status, along with whatever Volvo and Uber have opted to have recorded as status.

The processor memory of the on-board systems is another place to look. Once again, this presumes that those systems survived the crash (probably did so, since the crash impact did not seem to severely destroy the car), also whether or not the memory was intact, etc.

Another place to look is at any in-the-cloud system that communicates over-the-air with the self-driving car. This might or might not help, depending upon when the last communications with the car were, and what was captured from the self-driving car, and whether the cloud kept intact the data collected, etc.

As far as we know right now, the weather shouldn't be a factor in this incident, since it appears via the videos that there wasn't any rain (which could have made the roads slick), and there wasn't any snow (which could have obscured the sensors), etc. It appeared to be a typical Tempe evening, consisting of dry roads.

The video also suggests that other traffic was not a factor. It appears that there weren't other cars nearby during the incident. There doesn't appear to be any obstructions on the roadway, and so debris or other such factors don't seem to come to play in this case.

Scene Analysis

Let's do a scene analysis, based on what we know so far (again, all preliminary). See Figure 1.

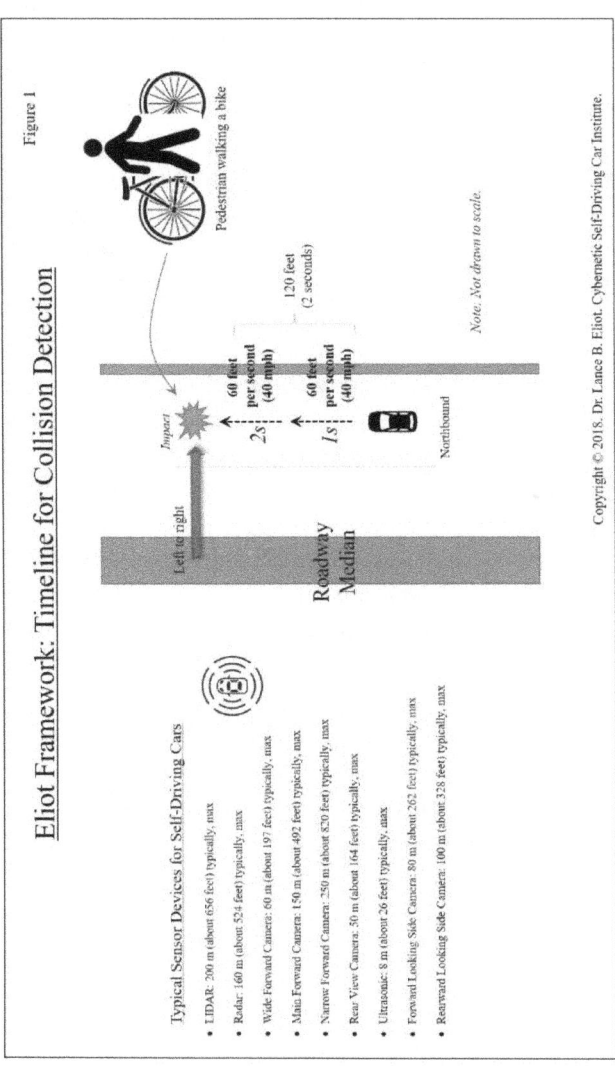

According to reports, the Uber self-driving car was heading northbound on North Mill Avenue. The incident occurred at a substantive distance prior to an intersection, and the pedestrian was walking a bicycle across the street, doing so illegally and jaywalking. The Uber self-driving car was reported as moving at 40 miles per hour, which is about the same as 60 feet per second. Some have said that the speed limit was 35, which implies that the Uber self-driving car was speeding, but others have said that the speed limit was 45, which would imply that the Uber self-driving car was abiding by the speed limit. I'll not address the speed limit issue herein at this time.

The northbound route at the juncture of the incident was apparently a two lane roadway that had a sizable median to the left, separating the northbound traffic from the southbound traffic. The median appears to have shrubs and trees, which we'll come back to in a few moments.

The Uber self-driving car appears to have been in the rightmost lane, and struck the pedestrian with the bicycle at a nearly direct head-on manner. The video seems to suggest that the Uber self-driving car was not braking and nor taking any kind of potential evasive action.

Per the video, it takes about 2 seconds from the time that the pedestrian and bicycle appear until the Uber self-driving cars strikes them. As shown in the diagram, I have placed the car at about 120 feet from the impact, which is presumably when the video suggests that visually the pedestrian and bicycle can be first seen by the camera. The official video is rather poorly illuminated, and it suggests that the area was relatively dark, but there is controversy over whether the on-board video was properly tuned to the lighting and whether the video sufficiently shows the actual lighting. Indeed, others have since the incident made their own videos by driving that same stretch at night, trying to showcase that it is much lighter there than was portrayed in the official video.

In any case, given a speed of 40 miles per hour, which is 60 feet per second, and since the video seems to suggest that from the point of being able to see the pedestrian and bicycle and to the impact that it was 2 seconds, we can guess that the distance was about 120 feet.

I show in the diagram the typical ranges for various kinds of sensors that are on self-driving cars. I'm not saying that these are the sensors that were on this particular self-driving car, and we'll need to find out what actual sensors were loaded into this self-driving car.

Generally, a wide forward camera has about a 197-foot maximum image collection capability. The lighting obviously makes a significant difference. Inadequate lighting can dramatically decrease that distance. There is some controversy about the headlights on the Uber self-driving car, since it seemed to only be able to cast light about 120 feet ahead, and yet we would normally expect headlights in proper working order to be able to shine ahead 160 feet (according to the NHTSA averages), and for a modern car perhaps even 200 to 220 feet. This is something that will need further exploration in this incident.

Some that saw the video were quick to say that the incident was "unavoidable" because they used solely the visual aspects to try and decide what was possible. This is what we would do if a human was driving a car. We know that humans have essentially only one form of sense to drive, their vision. Therefore, it would be easy to fall into the mental trap of assessing the situation by what a human driver does.

But, this is a self-driving car. As such, it is presumably loaded with lots of other kinds of sensors. As you can see from the Figure 1, LIDAR can detect about 656 feet (this is a form of light and radar), regular radar can do about 524 feet, and so even if the visual cameras weren't able to see anything sooner, these other sensors should have.

In essence, if the LIDAR and radar were on-board and working, and at a speed of 40 miles per hour for the self-driving car, the system should have had maybe 8-10 seconds of advance warning to have detected the pedestrian and bicycle. Now, I realize this is somewhat misleading because as far as we know the pedestrian was not just standing stationary there in the middle of the lane of the self-driving car.

We might assume that the pedestrian was over on the median and began to cross into the lanes of traffic, walking the bike as she was doing so. A normal walking speed is around 3.1 miles per hour, which is about 4.5 feet per second. The video seems to show her in the lane at the 2 seconds prior to the incident. We can deduce that if she was walking the bike, and we go backward in time, she presumably was on the median about 2-3 seconds sooner than when first seen in the video.

We would then say that the Uber self-driving car at 2-3 seconds sooner than when the camera sees her was perhaps another 120 to 180 feet back from the point at which the camera first spots her. We're now then at a distance of about 300 feet back from the point of impact.

What does this tell us? It suggests that even if the Uber self-driving car was back at 300 feet from the point of impact and the pedestrian was on the median and getting ready to go into the street, the distances for the radar and LIDAR to spot the pedestrian and the bicycle as they came into the street would still presumably be feasible, given the maximum distance capabilities of those devices.

Some have suggested that the shrubbery and trees on the median could have made it hard for the radar and LIDAR to distinguish the pedestrian and the bicycle. Yes, that's definitely an issue. They could either have been behind something that would have made the radar and LIDAR unlikely to spot them, or it could be that the nature of their structure made it hard.

Let me explain that aspect. If you train a neural network, which is considered a form of machine learning, you might feed it lots of images of pedestrians, and so it gradually trains on how to spot a pedestrian (via their image of having a body, legs, arms, a head, etc.). If you train a neural network on looking at bicycles, it can find patterns to be able to spot a bicycle, such as the tires, the handle bars, the seat, and so on.

If you combine together a pedestrian and a bicycle, it creates a new kind of image that is neither a pedestrian alone and nor a bike alone. Us humans can readily realize that a person standing in front of a bicycle is two kinds of objects, namely a pedestrian and a bicycle. A neural network that's not been trained for that image would not readily be able to realize what the combination is.

In essence, it is possible that even if the radar and LIDAR detected this "blob" consisting of a pedestrian and a bicycle, it was not logically able to determine what it was. This is crucial because if the AI was programmed to predict what might happen, and if it was established that a pedestrian could run into a street, or a bicycle could roll into a street, it might not have been able to discern what the intention of this blob was going to be.

Okay, let's assume that maybe it was a blob that the radar and LIDAR detected. Even if that's the case, it still would have been able to detect that the blob was moving. During those few seconds that the blob moved off the median, into the street, and then into the lane of the Uber self-driving car, it should still have been able to calculate that an object was moving into the oncoming path of the self-driving car. It might not have known what the blob was, but it could have at least determined that the blob was moving and moving into the path ahead.

Timeline of Collision Detection

Let's consider Figure 2.

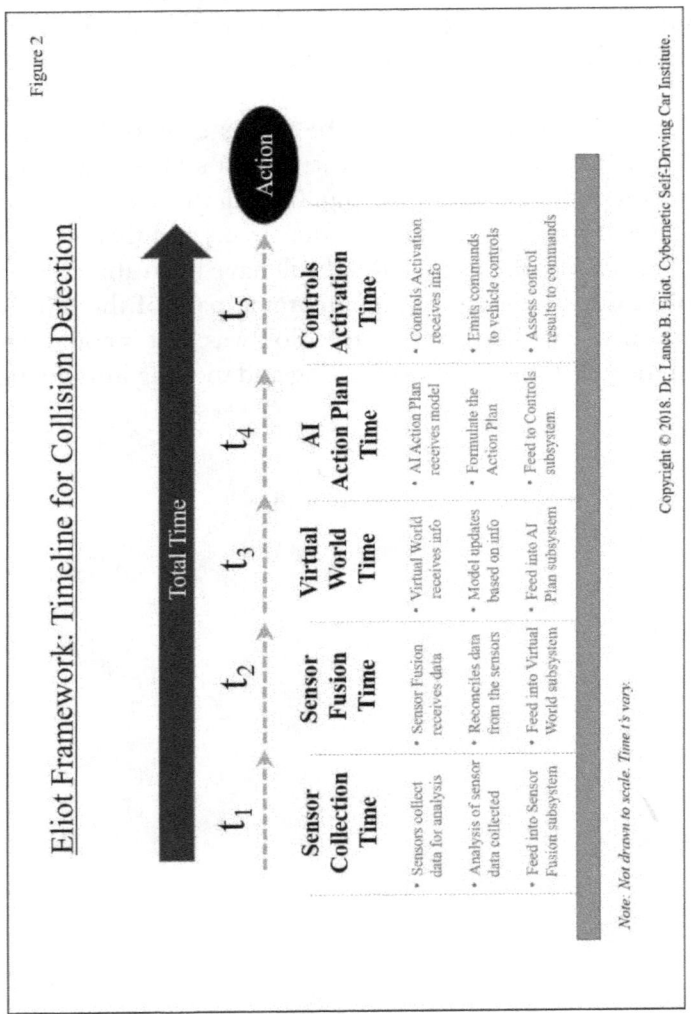

Some people have said that the moment that the self-driving car detected the pedestrian and bicycle, the AI should have instantaneously taken evasive action. Whoa! We need to consider that "time" is an element in any kind of system. Things don't just magically happen instantaneously.

As shown in Figure 2, there is a time involved in doing sensor data collection and analysis, let's call this amount of time to be known as t1. The sensor data and analysis get fed into the sensor fusion subsystem, which takes some amount of time to analyze all of the sensors together, and we'll call that amount of time to be t2. The sensor fusion analysis is fed into the virtual world model of the surrounding driving environment, and these updates take an amount of time t3. Then, the AI prepares an action plan based on what has been fed so far, and it takes some amount of time t4 for this to occur. Finally, the AI action plan flows to the controls activation subsystem, which takes some amount time t5 to send commands to the driving controls.

Therefore, we have Total Time = t1 + t2 + t3 + t4 + t5, which occurs prior to the driving control of the car doing anything other than what they were last told to do. In essence, if the self-driving car was doing 40 miles per hour, and the accelerator was set for that, and the brakes weren't being applied, and the steering was straight ahead, then until the Total Time occurs there won't be any new changes applied to the driving controls.

Studies of humans show that they typically take about 2.5 to 5 seconds to react to a sudden driving situation (from the point at which they first realize it), and it can be up to another 5-10 seconds before they fully take appropriate action to hit the brakes or steer the car. There is much debate about the norms of human reaction times in driving situations. Different people react differently, and different situations involve different reactions.

That being said, some studies claim that at a speed of 40 miles per hour that if a human realizes they need to stop the car on a suitable straightaway and they instantaneously jam on the brakes, the car itself could come to a stop in about 164 feet. This so-called stopping distance is a combination of "thinking time" (which would take about 76 feet) and "braking time" (about 88 feet), which, in this case implies that at the moment that the camera seems to reveal the pedestrian, if the brakes had ideally immediately been applied at the 2 second mark of 120 feet, and given that the roadway was a dry condition and seemingly well paved, and assuming the Uber self-driving car had good tires and good brakes, the Uber self-driving car would have had a slim chance of coming to a complete halt prior to the pedestrian but at least it would have struck the pedestrian with dramatically less force (likely leading to injury but not necessarily death); alternatively, the car could possibly have been steered away from the pedestrian while also hitting the brakes (causing no blow at all, or perhaps a glancing blow).

Keep in mind that these are all theoretical numbers at this stage of the analysis and we'll need to see what the official investigation shows as to the actual distances and actual times involved. I also advise that everyone be careful using the word "unavoidable" because as you can see from these numbers, there are "unavoidable" incidents that can have catastrophic results involving death, while there can be "unavoidable" incidents that might instead involve injury but not death.

Thus, if a human was actively driving the Uber self-driving car, and they were directly paying attention to the road, and if the video is accurately depicting that the pedestrian could not be seen other than the 2 seconds or so prior to impact, it seems unlikely that the human could have reacted in time to have completely stopped the car, though they might have been able to slow it. But, the video could be misleading, and an attentive human driver might have been able to see the pedestrian and bicycle on the median, and therefore had more time as a defensive driver to get ready to swerve or stop the car. Indeed, one might say that if the pedestrian had been without a bicycle, it might have been harder to spot her, but given the larger size of the "blob" by having both together, it would presumably have been easier to spot.

Furthermore, in the role as a back-up operator, in theory the human driver in the self-driving car is supposed to actively be watching for situations just like this. Unlike the average human driver that is just driving along in their own car, the back-up operator is purposely there to be aware and alert. And, they are supposed to be trained to do so. Unfortunately, what often happens is that the back-up operator becomes accustomed to nothing unusual happening, and so they become complacent. In this case, the inward pointing video shows that the back-up operator was looking down and away from the roadway. And glanced up just as the impact occurred.

Some of the self-driving car companies have two operators in their cars. One sits at the controls, while the other one sits in the back and is monitoring the status of the AI system. Presumably, the second operator sitting in the backseat can be acting to keep the operator in the front seat alert, doing so by watching them and urging them to stay alert. Some wonder whether Uber should have had a second human operator that could have been aiding the operator driving the vehicle to remain attentive. Others also wonder what kind of systems were in the car to try and keep the operator alert, such as systems that force the driver to keep their hands on the wheel, and systems that watch the eyes of the driver to make sure they are looking ahead.

In terms of the Total Time = t1 + t2 + t3 + t4 + t5, we don't yet know how long each of those steps took for this self-driving car. It depends on the speeds of the computer processors and the nature of the programming code and pattern matching systems, etc. The point is that the AI won't react "instantaneously" and instead it takes time to figure what is occurring and what to do about it.

Collision Detection Aspects

As shown in Figure 3, for self-driving cars there are right now an AI system that serves as the primary driver, and a human operator that serves as the secondary or back-up driver.

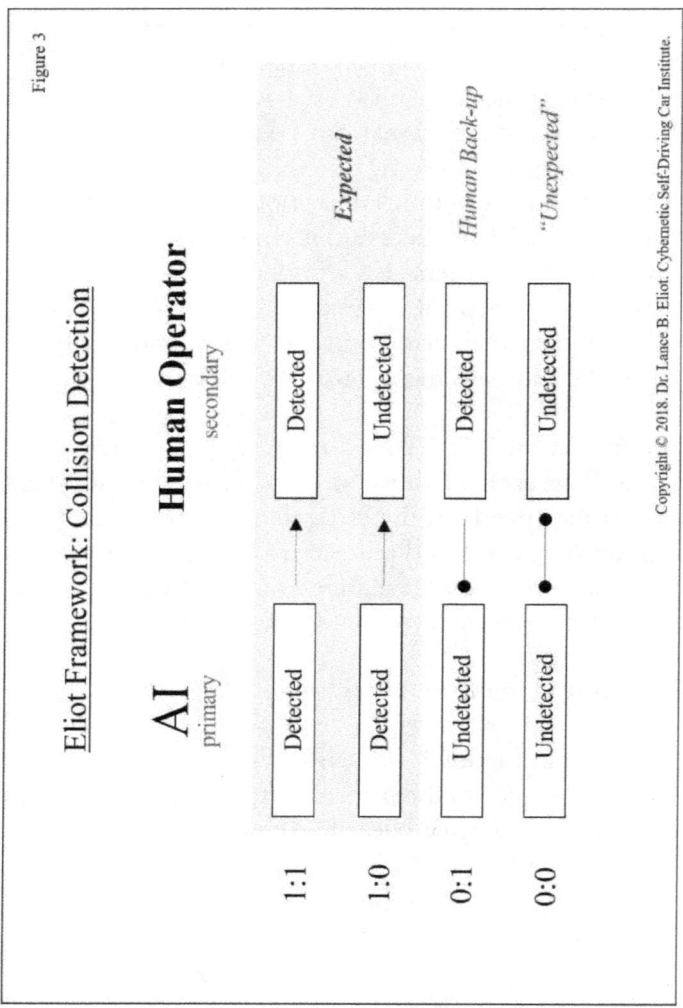

Figure 3

Eliot Framework: Collision Detection

What's supposed to happen is that the AI system detects a potential collision, and possibly the human back-up operator does too, but presumably the AI system will take the needed action and the back-up operator just goes along for the ride in that use case.

There's also the circumstance of the AI making a detection of a possible collision, and the human back-up operator does not, in which case the AI system takes the needed action and the back-up operator is fortunate that the AI figured out what to do.

The not-so-good case is when the AI does not detect a potential collision. In theory, the back-up operator than takes over the controls, assuming they detect the upcoming collision. This is not as easy as it sounds. The human back-up operator might be reluctant to take over the controls and unsure of whether a potential collision is really going to happen and can become over-confident in the AI system.

The worst-case scenario is when the AI doesn't detect the potential collision and nor does the human back-up operator.

It seems that's what happened in the Uber self-driving car instance in Tempe.

Take a look at Figure 4.

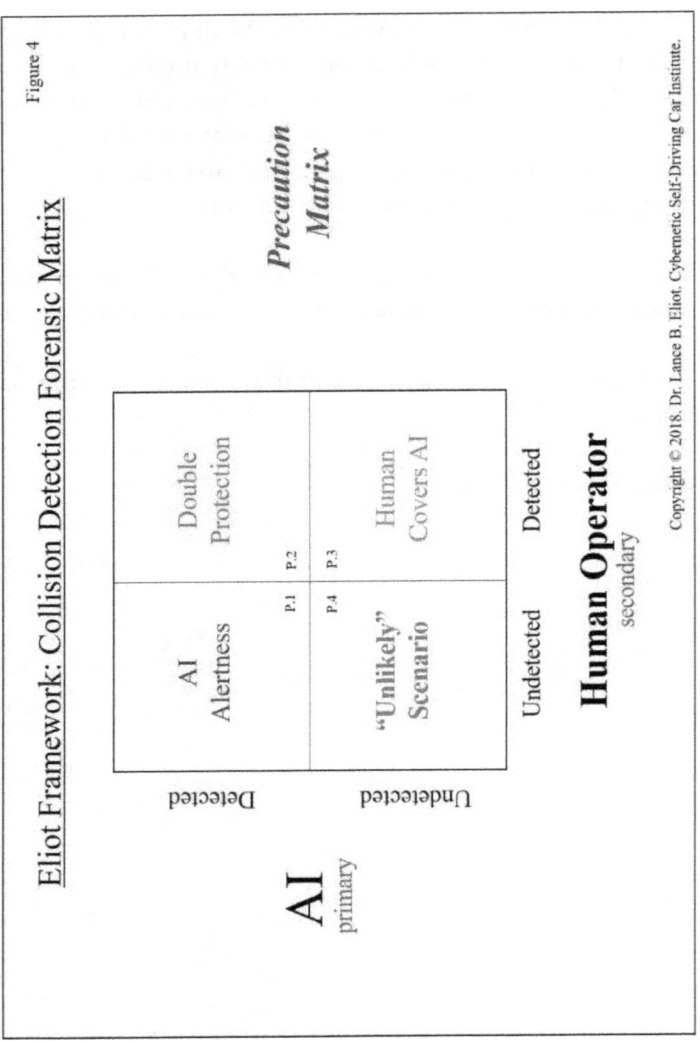

Figure 4

Eliot Framework: Collision Detection Forensic Matrix

Precaution Matrix

In the upper right corner of the Collision Detection Forensic Matrix, labeled as box P.2, we have the double protection of both the AI and the human operator detecting a potential collision. This is what we want to happen.

The upper left corner shows the instance of when the AI makes the detection, but the human operator does not, and it's what we also expect to have happen from time-to-time (labeled as P.1), namely that the AI has more advanced sensory capabilities and alertness than does a human, and so it should presumably be able to do a better job at detecting potential collisions. That's the theory of it.

But, we know that today the AI is not fully at a human driver functioning capacity, and so we have the human operator there to serve as a back-up, and so the lower right corner (P.3) shows the instance when the human covers for the AI.

The toughest scenario of them all is in the lower left corner, labeled as P.4. This is the circumstance wherein the AI doesn't detect a collision and nor does the human back-up operator. I know that many of the auto makers and tech firms say that this "should never happen," but that's wishful thinking. We seem to have a now well-publicized case in which it did happen. And, as I've predicted, we'll have more.

No-Evasive-Action Matrix

Figure 5 shows the No-Evasive-Action Failure Matrix.

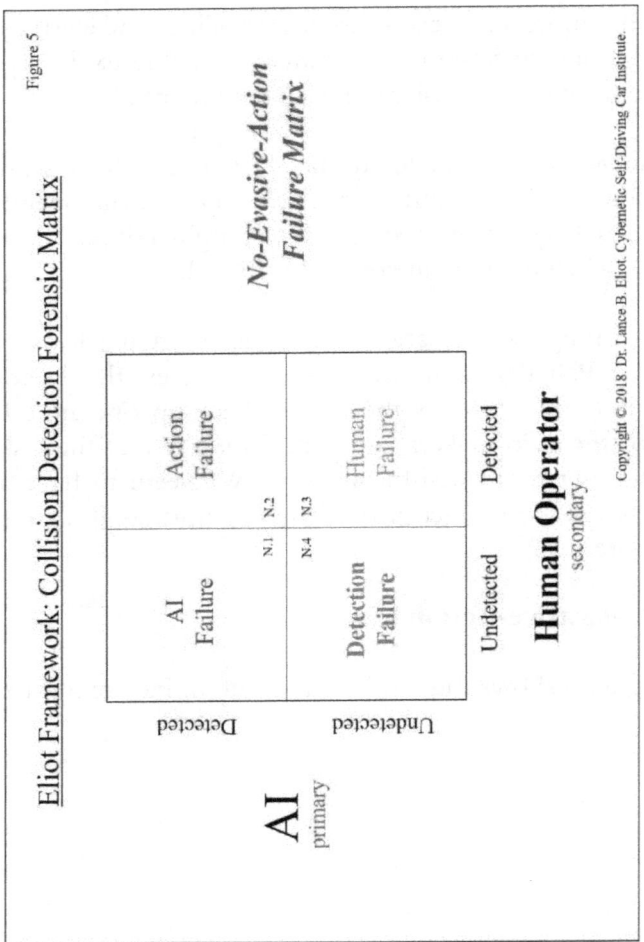

Figure 5

Eliot Framework: Collision Detection Forensic Matrix

No-Evasive-Action Failure Matrix

Copyright © 2018 Dr. Lance B. Eliot. Cybernetic Self-Driving Car Institute.

If a self-driving car opts to not take any evasive action, neither done by the AI and nor by the human operator, we need to consider how this might have occurred.

There are four scenarios.

If the AI detected a collision upcoming, and the human back-up operator did so too, but if neither took any evasive action, we would have essentially a catastrophic action failure (box N.2). It could be vexing to think that neither the AI and nor the human took evasive action, even though they both detected that a collision was imminent.

If the AI detected a collision upcoming, and the human did not, and yet the AI did not take evasive action, we'd say that AI failed to do something even though it detected the collision (box N.1). If the human detected a collision upcoming, and the AI did not, and yet the human did not take evasive action, we'd say that the human failed to do something even though they detected the collision (box N.3). Finally, if both failed to detect, it pretty much stands to reason that no evasive action would be taken, and so we'd want to know why neither of them detected the collision.

You might be wondering why the AI might not detect a potential collision.

Take a look at Figure 6 to see a Collision Detection Forensic Tree.

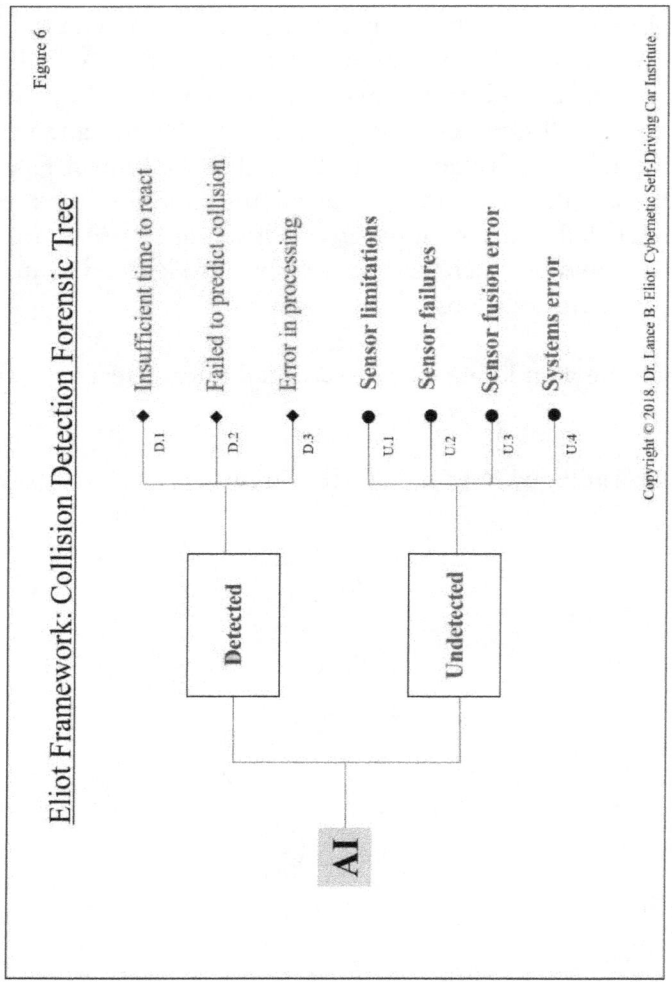

Figure 6

Eliot Framework: Collision Detection Forensic Tree

Copyright © 2018. Dr. Lance B. Eliot. Cybernetic Self-Driving Car Institute.

As shown, let's consider the circumstance of the AI detecting a potential collision, but it didn't take evasive action. It could be that there was insufficient time to react (labeled as D.1). If the Uber self-driving car actually spotted the pedestrian at the 2 seconds to impact, and if the t1+t2+t3+t4+t5 took let's say 3 seconds, it would imply that the AI was midstream of detection and had not yet sent commands to the controls of the car to take action. Therefore, from all outside appearances, it would look like the AI did nothing at all. In actuality, it might have been in the midst of deciding what to do.

Another possibility is that the AI detected the pedestrian and the bicycle but failed to predict that a collision would occur (labeled as D.2). Maybe the AI calculated that the "blob" was not going to intersect into its lane, or that they would pass through the lane and so no action was needed. From outside appearances, we don't know if the AI actively decided that the prudent course was to continue ahead and did so because there didn't seem to be a collision arising.

There might have also been an error in the processing of the AI. Perhaps it was updating the virtual world model, and there's an error in that part of the system that led to the placement of the pedestrian and bicycle further away from the lane. Or, maybe the AI action plan had no prior programming to cope with a circumstance like this, and so it was not able to come up with an evasive plan. From outside appearances, we don't know if the inner workings of the AI might have made errors as it was undertaking t1, t2, t3, t4, t5.

There's another twist to this too.

Suppose the AI did detect the pedestrian and bicycle, but classified the two as a blob, and therefore considered it to be an unknown object. Maybe it had no clue as to what it was and just only surmised that there was something there. As such, another option would be to try and decide whether to do an emergency braking, or instead just drive through whatever it is. This is akin to when you sometimes see an tumbleweed on the roadway and maybe you decide that it is safer for you to just hit the tumbleweed, rather than doing a dangerous braking or swerving, or maybe you believe there is insufficient time to take any evasive action and so you just proceed ahead. From outside appearances, we only seem to know that the self-driving car proceeded ahead unabated, but it could have been a misguided intentional act under the assumption that there was just some kind of debris in the roadway and thus seemingly the best course of action was to strike it.

The other part of this tree is the part that involves the AI not detecting the pedestrian and bicycle.

This could have happened due to limitations of the sensors that were on this particular self-driving car (U.1), or it could be that the sensors failed (U.2). For example, suppose the LIDAR was not working correctly or had some malady during the time that it was scanning in that area, and the same for the radar. Now, presumably, the importance of having multiple sensors and of different types is that when one of them falters or fails, the others are there to help take up the slack.

The sensor fusion could have made an error (U.3). Suppose the LIDAR reported that it didn't detect the pedestrian, while the radar did. How was the sensor fusion programmed? It might have been programmed that if the LIDAR doesn't vote the same way as the radar, it considers the circumstance as a false reading by the radar. And, so the sensor fusion ignores the radar. If you then also add to this calculation that maybe it is programmed to wait and see what the cameras spot, you could easily get down to those last 2 seconds, in that the sensor fusion might have been deciding that the radar and LIDAR weren't aligned with each other and it was going to therefore wait until the camera said something.

There could be other systems errors that could have led to the lack of a detection (labeled as U.4). Keep in mind that there are a myriad of subsystems involved in a self-driving car, and likely millions of lines of programming code. Even with this being tested by lots of simulations, the auto makers and tech firms are saying that they cannot really test everything until they put these cars onto the roadways. There could be some other aspect internally that prevented the detection.

Human Operator Aspects

Take a look at Figure 7 to consider what occurs about the human operator and detection of a collision.

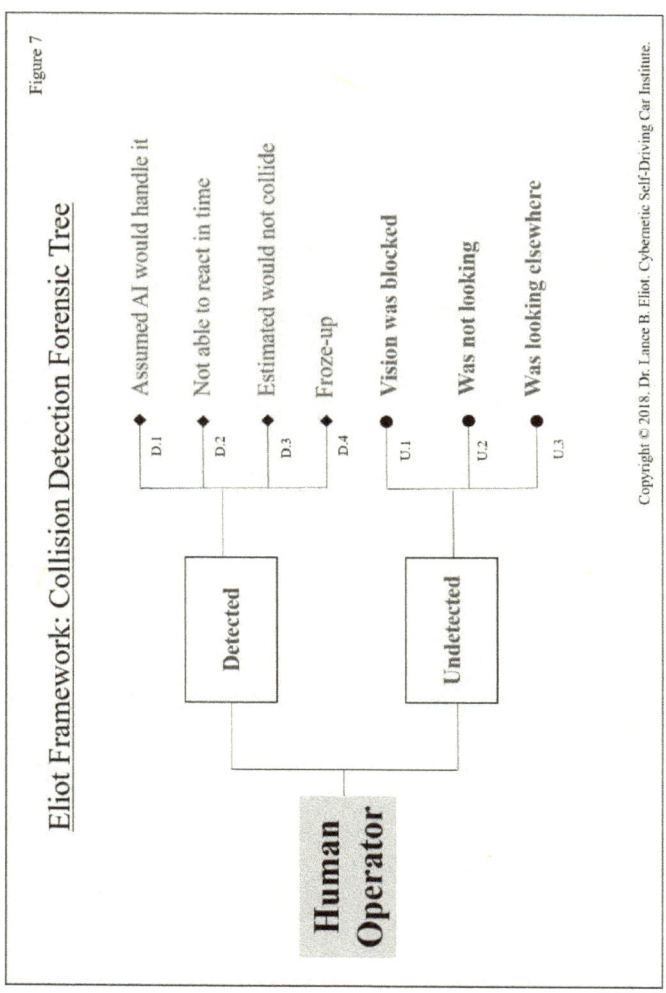

Figure 7

Eliot Framework: Collision Detection Forensic Tree

Copyright © 2018. Dr. Lance B. Eliot. Cybernetic Self-Driving Car Institute.

Suppose the human operator does detect a potential collision but opts to not take evasive action. Why would this be?

It could be that the human back-up operator assumed the AI would handle it (D.1). It could be that they weren't able to react in time (D.2). It could be that they estimated there would not be an actual collision (D.3). Or, they might have just frozen up, maybe startled at what was going to happen (D.4).

Suppose the human operator did not detect a potential collision. How can this be?

It could be that their vision was blocked (U.1). It could be that they weren't looking (U.2). It could be that they were looking elsewhere (U.3).

According to the inward facing video, the human operator in this case seemed to be looking downward at something, so we'd call this a U.3 instance of looking elsewhere, and they were not looking at the roadway for those crucial moments and so they are also doing a U.2 (not looking).

Lessons To Be Learned
Overall, it's still early to figure out what actually happened.

But, I hope that we learn so far at least these lessons:

- AI is not infallible, and we should not anthropomorphize it into being all-knowing

- People developed the AI and so we need to consider what the system was developed to do

- We need to hold accountable the companies that made the AI and not shrug it off as just "woeful systems"

- There is no such thing as zero fatalities with self-driving cars, not now, not ever

- Self-driving cars are a combination of hardware and software, all of which can falter

- Human back-up operators will become complacent and we need to minimize this

- Reaction times for AI systems need to be determined and tuned to optimal levels

- What happens with one particular self-driving car model can occur similarly in others

- Finding and fixing one potential error or bug does not ergo mean that the AI is now perfected

- Other self-driving car models are just as likely to have other kinds of issues or errors, so don't become fixated on one issue that happens to have first arisen with great visibility

And, we need to increase the importance of safety as a key factor in the design, development, and fielding of self-driving cars. This needs to be a mantra for all stakeholders and for all parts of the industry.

CHAPTER 8
POWER CONSUMPTION
AND
SELF-DRIVING CARS

CHAPTER 8

POWER CONSUMPTION AND
SELF-DRIVING CARS

I was in an airport and on my way to give a speech about self-driving cars when I realized that my smartphone was getting low on its battery charge and I knew that the flight itself would not have any power outlets at the seats. I looked around the gate area to see if there was a place to plug-in my phone to charge it. Most airports seem to have charging bars where you can plug-in your phone, but this airport was apparently stuck in the 1980s and there weren't any designated areas for phone charging. My next plan of attack was to find an electrical outlet, preferably one that was near some seats so that I could sit down and be right next to my phone as it was getting charged up.

Disappointedly, this airport wasn't just in the 1980s and instead, worse still, was in the Neanderthal era because there weren't any electrical outlets anywhere. In fact, it almost seemed like the airport had purposely tried to hide or close-off any chances of finding an electrical outlet. There were some desperate business people that had reached behind a candy dispensing vending machine and had plugged in their phones there (they even had worked together to push the vending machine a few inches from the wall to then get access to the precious electrical outlets behind it). I was getting desperate as my smartphone dropped below 10% and at any moment it would be entirely without power.

I turned it off to preserve what I considered "emergency energy" in the battery and continued my search. After walking endlessly in the airport, I finally decided there wasn't any place available to charge my phone, and had a revelation that I could use my laptop to charge my phone. It meant though that I'd be depleting my laptop charge, but it was worth it to get my smartphone back into the green zone of available charge.

I'm sure that you've encountered similar dilemmas of trying to find a place to charge your smartphone and having to be cognizant of how much battery you've got left to go. In my case, it was admittedly not a life-or-death matter as to whether I had a well-charged phone or not -- in theory, I could have just gotten onto the flight and slept the whole way to my destination. Like most people, I just feel better to know that my phone is charged and ready for use. Without a charged-up phone, it's almost as though I had left my wallet at home and would miss being able to use my smartphone, as much as missing having my wallet with me. You might say I am overly dependent on my smartphone, but I dare say there are a lot of people that feel the same way about having a charged and usable smartphone with them.

There are some occasions where the amount of battery charge in an electrical device of some kind could be a life-or-death matter. A notable scene in the movie "Apollo 13" showcased a famous life-or-death moment when the astronauts on the Apollo 13 space craft had to deal with a dicey situation involving electrical power and battery charges. The day was April 13, 1970 and the Apollo 13 spacecraft was over 321,000 kilometers on the way to the moon, when unexpectedly one of their oxygen tanks exploded, they no longer could produce electricity with their service module fuel cells (those cells needed oxygen to aid in producing electrical power).

The astronauts and NASA ground control realized in those tense moments that they would need to quickly power down the spacecraft and try to conserve power. This was especially important since they would need sufficient power leftover to run the spacecraft once they were getting back toward earth. If they didn't have enough power remaining by the end of the trip, they'd likely die as they tried to make that last step to get back here. Powering down though meant they would need to operate without much power during the bulk of the return trip, and this included not being able to run the heaters in the spacecraft (turns out, this led to the interior of the spacecraft becoming bone chillingly cold and dangerously wet, which is not a normally prudent approach and is illustrative of how desperate the situation had become).

Even the power-up sequence had to be carefully orchestrated. Down on earth at NASA there was a scramble to use the spacecraft simulator to figure out the best power-up procedure for the astronauts to use. Different sequences would consume differing amounts of battery charge. By experimenting with a myriad of sequences, they were able to find a series of steps that would help to minimize the electrical charge consumed at reboot. As you know, fortunately the Apollo 13 crew was able to get home and it turned out to be an incredible indication of the savviness of our space efforts that such a dire situation was successfully overcome. Sidenote: If you do a search on the web for historical documents about the Apollo 13 mission, you can find a copy of the actual notes that the astronauts made on their spacecraft instruction manual as they were dealing with the power issue.

I freely admit that whether my smartphone has a sufficient charge or not would probably be less consequential than what the Apollo 13 crew faced, but nonetheless the amount of battery on my smartphone is important to me. We all tend to watch our smartphones and keep aware of how much charge we have left at any time. On a related topic, here's an interesting question for you, do you pay attention to how much battery charge there is in your car? In other words, do you put as much attention to the charge of your car battery as you do of your car phone? I'd dare say that if you drive a gasoline powered car that you rarely think about your car battery charge. You just assume that your car battery is working and properly charged. Until you have a moment where you try to start your car and it won't start and makes that irritating noise like the battery is dead, you assume the battery is good.

In contrast, those of you that have an electrical car, you are likely aware of the battery charge in your car. You need to make sure that you have sufficient charge to go wherever it is you are aiming to go. This requires knowing how much total charge capacity your battery has, how long it takes to charge it, and know of places that you can stop to get a charge. Now, I don't want to overstate this aspect since I realize that electrical car owners point out that you can argue the same thing about gasoline powered cars -- gas powered car drivers need to know how much gas is in the car tank, they need to know how miles they can go on the remaining gas, and they need to know where they can find a gas station to fill-up.

For a conventional electric car, some drivers even try to help reduce the power consumption by turning off their infotainment system and their air conditioning whenever they get toward the last trickle of electricity left in their car battery (yes, gasoline powered car drivers often do the same to reduce gas usage). The amount of charge available determines the distance an electric car can drive, and no one wants to get stuck on the roadways with a car out-of-charge (akin to being out-of-gas). I guess we all face our own Apollo 13 moments when driving our cars, having to be aware of either our remaining battery charge or our remaining gasoline amount.

What does this have to do with AI self-driving cars?

At the Cybernetic Self-Driving Car Institute, we are exploring ways to conserve power consumption via the AI of the self-driving car. Just as the Apollo 13 ground crew and spacecraft crew figured out how to best use their electrical power, the AI of the self-driving car can be doing likewise.

You might be wondering why electrical power for a self-driving car is an issue at all.

Here's why.

For an AI self-driving car, there needs to be an abundance of specialized sensors on the car to be able to sense the world, including video cameras, radar units, ultrasonic units, LIDAR, and so on. Each of these are electrical devices that consume electrical power. Furthermore, the AI needs lots of computer processors and on-board computer memory, and other related electrical devices, all of which consume electrical power. In essence, you need a miniature power plant to be able to operate all of the add-on's that make an AI self-driving car into being an AI self-driving car.

For any conventional car, electrical or gasoline, you need electrical power to do the normal things for powering a car, including providing start-up power to get the engine going, power for the infotainment system, power for the headlights and signals of the car, etc. That's a fair amount of power right there. Plus, people are nowadays expecting to plug their smartphones into their car and often use laptops too, all of which consume more power. Then, we're adding a huge additional layer of automation and electrically powered devices to do the self-driving of the car. An AI self-driving car becomes one big power-hungry rolling monster.

For Level 5 self-driving cars, which are ones that need no human driver and the AI is supposed to be able drive in whatever manner a human can drive, we are anticipating that the human occupants in the self-driving car will likely be consuming power in new ways. One concept is that the inside of the self-driving car might have large LED displays throughout the inner walls of the car, allowing people to watch movies while the AI drives the car for them. Various interactive devices like laptops, but maybe something beyond laptops and that hasn't been invented yet, will be inside the self-driving car for purposes of work or play. Nobody really knows yet what the inside of the futuristic AI self-driving car will be, but you can pretty much bet that whatever it is will require the consumption of electrical power.

Some even say that the exterior of the self-driving car will also have electronic displays. We might have outside electronic boards that help communicate to other drivers what our self-driving car is doing, such as it might display that it wants to get over into the next lane. Or, the electronic displays might be used for advertising purposes and the owner of the self-driving car could make extra money by agreeing to have ads displayed. As an aside, there are others that say this doesn't make much sense because people will be working or playing inside the cocoon of their self-driving car and will rarely if ever look outside. If they aren't looking outside, they won't see ads being displayed on the outside of other cars (though, pedestrians could see it, admittedly).

Anyway, there's pretty much no disagreement that AI self-driving cars are going to crave electrical power.

Until we invent some other novel power source, all of these needed devices are going to be consuming electricity. It's as though you need a nuclear power plant inside of your AI self-driving car. That being said, you might at first glance assume that an all-electric car would somehow then be the best candidate for AI self-driving cars, since it's all about producing electrical power.

Ironically, there is a view that a hybrid car is maybe the better choice for AI self-driving cars.

The belief is based on the idea that in case you run out of electrical power to run the car, you can at least switch over to the gasoline and keep your car going for a while. Not everyone buys into this logic. They say that if you consider the gasoline as though it is a virtual reserve of electrical power, why shouldn't you just do the same as to your actual battery and electrical power? In other words, just make sure to keep the same amount of electrical power in reserve. One counter-argument is that the ability to get gasoline is generally much easier today, since there are gas stations on almost every street corner, while electrical charging stations and locations are scarce. This might change in the future, but for today, certainly it is relatively easier to get gas than it is to get your car charged.

I'll add fuel to the fire, so to speak, and point out too that AI self-driving cars are anticipated to be running much often than conventional cars. For conventional cars, you drive it to work and leave it sitting in a parking lot for hours on end. You drive it home, and leave it sitting for hours on end in your garage. The odds are that a conventional car is really only used just a few scant hours of the day. Most of the time, your car is doing nothing.

With AI self-driving cars, the belief is that you'll put your self-driving car to use all day long, each day, for a usage of near to 24x7.

When you are at work, you'll hire out your AI self-driving car as a ride sharing service. When you are at home sleeping, your self-driving car will be out making money for you doing nighttime ride sharing. You might also use your self-driving car to do errands for you, such as sending your self-driving car over to the grocery, where the store clerks have pre-assembled your ordered items and are ready to place them into your car, which your obedient self-driving car then dutifully brings those groceries back home to you.

If your self-driving car is continually on the move and going all day long, it means more power consumption than a conventional car, by far, and also raises the issue of how will your AI self-driving car be able to keep charged-up. Presumably, we'll have gas stations and charging stations that will accommodate self-driving cars, including ones that have no human occupants inside at the time the self-driving car comes to do a fill-up. There might at first be human attendants at the gas and charging stations, but we will ultimately likely see unattended stations, meaning that your unattended AI self-driving car can go into an unattended gas station or charging station and fill-up without any needed human intervention.

The experimental AI self-driving cars that are being tested on roadways are prone to the same issue of consuming a whole lot of electrical power, and so you might assume that they've figured out how to deal with the power consumption crunch. Not really. Many of these experimental self-driving cars are not being run all day long, they are running at only low speeds, they are used only for short trips, and otherwise being used in a manner which is contrary to what will likely happen once they are released into the wild. Furthermore, they are adroitly pampered by the auto maker or tech firm and so we don't hear about the power consumption issue (they have an entire human pit crew at-the-ready).

If you are a self-driving car that has a dedicated team of engineers, they are taking care of the power aspects and no one else would realize that the power might be a problematic aspect. Once these cars get into the hands of consumers, the consumer perception of having to deal with the power consumption could potentially undermine their joy for these electricity gulping vehicles.

Another twist involves the over-the-air (OTA) updates that are anticipated to be needed for AI self-driving cars. There is a communications capability included in most AI self-driving cars that allows for the AI system to communicate with a cloud-based system setup by the auto maker or tech firm. The self-driving car uploads data and the cloud downloads data and programs into the self-driving car. For some of the self-driving cars, they are made to mainly do this only when the self-driving car is sitting still, stopped, and when the car is not being charged. This will cut into the available time for charging the self-driving car.

By the way, there's another angle to these many electrical devices on your self-driving car, namely the heat issue.

You might have used a laptop that generated heat while it was running, doing so lightly when the laptop was under minimal use, and then getting quite hot when playing that latest online game and really exercising the processor and electrical components. Imagine that your self-driving car has all of these exotic electrical devices for radar, cameras, and the like, and the numerous computer processors too, and when they are all going full blast it generates a tremendous amount of heat. The self-driving car has to be designed to properly dissipate the heat, otherwise the electrical devices will fry. You can't afford to have your radar unit fry out while the self-driving car is hurtling down the freeway at 80 miles per hour. Ironically, the systems that will dissipate the heat often require electrical power themselves and thus consumer more of the battery of the self-driving car.

There's also a question of where to put all of these various AI self-driving car devices. Some of the devices need to go in certain areas of the self-driving car. For example, the cameras need a clear line of sight and are mounted at the front, sides, and back of the car. The processors and related electrical devices can be mounted elsewhere in the car, but you can only hide them in so many places, and right now some auto makers are putting these processors into the trunk.

Consumers though aren't going to be happy with a self-driving car that has zero trunk space.

Overall, as much as possible, the self-driving car makers are going to need to find ways to reduce the amount of electrical power consumption. You might counter argue that we just need to increase the ability of the self-driving car to generate and store electrical power, which certainly is an equally strident goal, and so in that case it doesn't really matter how much power is consumed. A self-driving car that has a tremendous sized battery and an ability to generate power while underway will help to mitigate the power consumption problem. Advances in car design, battery design, and electrical power generation in cars is ongoing and I'm sure we'll gradually see improvements.

I don't think though that we can wait for that to happen, and we must meanwhile assume that we need to find ways to conserve power in the AI self-driving car. You can liken this to smartphones. Early smartphones were battery hogs and only had small batteries. Power management became a big topic of how to decrease the smartphone use of power. Meanwhile, batteries got better. But, at the same time, smartphones got more features and increased how much power they use. It's an ongoing cat-and-mouse game, improving the batteries and how power is consumed, and the two will go hand-in-hand in the same manner for AI self-driving cars.

One of the most obvious ways to try and reduce power consumption is the nature of the electrical devices themselves that are on the self-driving car. Few of the makers for the radar units, cameras, and other sensory devices have been pushed hard on the power consumption issue up until now, and the push has been mainly for those devices to get better at what they do and get smaller in size. The smaller size is good for self-driving cars since it reduces typically the weight and the bulk of where it will sit in the car. Gradually the power consumption issue has become a bigger issue that they are trying to solve.

Same can be said about the computer processors and memory on-board of the self-driving car. We already know that for purposes of making laptops lighter and smaller, there has been a push towards processors and memory that are smaller and use less power. Nvidia recently produced an 8-core CPU that they claim can do 30 TOPS (trillion operations per second) and only consume 30 watts (called Xavier), and they have another processor that supposedly does 320 TOPS at 500 watts (it's called Pegasus), all especially earmarked for AI self-driving cars. These kinds of advances are encouraging signs of reducing the electrical power needs of a self-driving car.

One of the ways that some are now describing the power consumption of the AI self-driving car is to liken it to some approximated number of laptops. In other words, suppose your AI self-driving car had (let's say) 50 to 100 laptops that were all working at the same time and at their peak energy needs and were inside of your AI self-driving car. That provides an overall sense of the magnitude of the amount of power being consumed just for the AI and self-driving car aspects of the car.

As mentioned earlier, one hope for reducing the power consumption involves having the device makers try to design the devices to use as little power as possible. Another variation of this idea would be to have the device itself moderate how much power that it needs. In essence, have a device that is "smart" and knows when it can reduce its power consumption. Again, somewhat similar to what our laptops today do, your laptop goes into a sleep mode when it thinks there's a moment to do so, cutting down on its power use, and then wakes up when it needs to do so.

For example, you might have processors on the self-driving car that go into a sleep mode, reducing their power consumption. They then kick back into use once the processors need to do something. We could try the same trick with the sensor devices. Maybe the radar unit for example goes into sleep mode, reducing its power consumption, and then when needed it wakes-up and at that time the power consumption rises.

On paper, this seems like a good idea. In reality, have you had your laptop go into sleep mode and then it balks sometimes at waking up? Imagine if your self-driving car is going along the highway at 65 miles per hour and the radar decides to go to sleep because it hasn't been used in the last few milliseconds. Great, a tiny savings on electrical consumption. But, then suppose the radar is urgently awoken, but freezes up, just when it is needed to detect that a large truck might be veering toward the self-driving car. Do you want your life dependent upon an electrical device that maybe or maybe not can come out of sleep mode? It's unnerving, for sure. However this is to be undertaken, it needs to be smartly managed.

Can the AI itself help with the power consumption issue?

We believe that the AI can and indeed should be involved in the power consumption solution.

Let's start with the idea of a device that is "smart" enough to do its own power management. If you allow an individual device to decide whether it can go into a sleep mode, the device itself might or might not choose a good time to do so. The AI of the self-driving car will have a better idea of when it might or might not need a particular device to be working. It is the AI that has the overall plan of what the self-driving car is doing and what it will do next. Individual devices usually do not have that wide of a scope of awareness, and are only focused on their specific task at-hand.

Therefore, it makes sense to have the AI aid in determining when a specific device can take a siesta, one might say, and reduce its power consumption. The AI then also has to be smart enough to realize how this blinds or otherwise adversely impacts the self-driving car. And, the AI needs to be aware of how long it will take to wake-up the device and reengage the device.

The point here is that the AI must do power management in a savvy manner. It cannot just arbitrarily start telling devices to shut down or go into low power modes. Instead, the AI has to be determining when to have any device do its power consuming efforts, and what impact it has to the driving mission and journey. Plus, the AI must anticipate the likely amount of time that will be required for the device to wake-up and function, and be calculating the odds that maybe the device doesn't wake-up in time and so have contingency plans in case it does not.

Also, the AI must know what kind of power consumption each device has, along with in what circumstances it uses that power. Shutting down momentarily five tiny power consumers might not be as advantageous as shutting down a single power consuming hog. There are some devices too that the AI might rarely if ever allow to shut down because they are mission critical to the driving task, and others of a lesser importance that it is willing to shut down all the time during a driving journey.

Having the AI be able to do this is considered an "edge" problem by most of the auto makers and tech firms. An edge problem is one that is not considered as core to the driving task of the self-driving car. It is a lesser important task. In this case, the power consumption is not yet perceived by most of the auto makers and tech firms as a significant problem, which is true because as mentioned earlier these self-driving cars aren't in the hands of consumers as yet, and so the AI to do this power management is not yet being given much attention. Ultimately, it will need to get attention.

What makes this somewhat tricky too is that the devices themselves are being constantly updated and improved. Thus, if the AI was setup for device X and power management aspects about it, and then you replace that device X with a device Y, and maybe the device Y has different power consumption aspects than did device X, you need to then have the AI adjust accordingly.

Another important factor to keep in mind involves the interaction between the AI and the device. The device might have its own power management capabilities. It should be informing the AI about what it wants to do about power management. The AI then can either agree or disagree. The two would need to negotiate as to what should take place. Meanwhile, the AI might instigate an indication to the device that it can go ahead and shift into low power mode. The device might have some reason why it thinks doing so is not sensible at that time, and so it might let the AI know that it disagrees with the command. This kind of give-and-take between the device and the AI will need to be fluid in nature and figured out as to how these kinds of discussions or arguments are to be settled.

If you include the fact that the self-driving car might have dozens upon dozens of electrical devices, the AI could get preoccupied by the power management aspects. And, of course, the AI itself is using up processors and on-board memory to undertake the power management task, which again uses up more electrical power. On the balance, though, the AI should be saving more than enough power by the power management overall, such that the overhead of doing the power management is worthwhile for the power conservation efforts.

Generally, too, the top priority for the AI still involves driving the car, and so the power management is considered a secondary task in comparison to the driving task. A self-driving car that has done a tremendous job of minimizing power consumption, but that runs into a wall because the AI was not paying attention to the driving task, well, that's not an astute way to design an AI self-driving car. The AI for power management is a separate but integrated module for the overarching framework of the AI of the self-driving car. It would work relatively independently of the rest of the AI, though tap into the rest of the AI as part of the essentials of knowing what the self-driving car is up to, and therefore how and when the devices on the self-driving car need to be in full working status.

Electric cars have had battery packs of about 24 kWatt-hours that allowed for less than 100 hundred miles on a full-charge, and then they shifted toward 60 kWatt-hours capacity batteries allowing for maybe 200 miles ranges, and some are in the 100 kWatt-hours capacity allowing for just over a 300 mile range. James Watt, for whom the electrical consumption unit was named, would probably be flattered to know that for modern and futuristic AI self-driving cars that we are still thinking about electrical power aspects. We do indeed need to find ways to increase the power producing and power storing capabilities of self-driving cars, and find ways to reduce power consuming aspects of the devices and systems, if we want to have true AI self-driving car.

We hopefully won't get ourselves into an electrical power bind – imagine that while in an AI self-driving car, one that lacks AI for power management, the AI suddenly announces to you, a human occupant inside the self-driving car, it cannot go much further because it is about to run out of power. Suppose further that this happens while the self-driving car is on the freeway going 80 miles per hour, and that the power will run out in the next five seconds.

Yikes!

I doubt that allowing the AI to tap into our personal laptop to draw power, in order to make it over that next bridge or take that exit off the freeway, will be a reassuring means of power management. There is a better way.

CHAPTER 9
ROAD RAGE
AND
SELF-DRIVING CARS

CHAPTER 9

ROAD RAGE AND SELF-DRIVING CARS

Have you ever experienced road rage?

Most of us have at one time or another have experienced a road rage act imposed upon us or perhaps even internally felt our own burning sensation of road rage (thankfully, most drivers do not seem to overtly act out on it). Here in Los Angeles, we hold the distinction of originally coining the phrase "road rage" when a local reporter opted to describe a series of untoward driving and attack events that had occurred on our freeways by saying it amounted to an eruption of "road rage."

According to the National Highway Traffic Safety Administration (NHTSA), road rage involves a driver that "commits moving traffic offenses so as to endanger other persons or property; an assault with a motor vehicle or other dangerous weapon by the operator or passenger of one motor vehicle on the operator or passengers of another motor vehicle." Some dictionary definitions say that it is an uncontrollable urge or impulse, but I don't like the use of the word "uncontrollable" being used because it suggests that the perpetrators are somehow being forced to perform such acts by an invisible hand, when in fact they could prevent their acts by exerting better self-control.

A research study done in 2016 reported that based on a survey of United States drivers, about 80% indicated they had experienced either road rage, significant anger, or overt aggression, at least once in the last year while driving on the roadways. Nearly half said they had experienced purposeful tailgating, and slightly less than half indicated they had either yelled at another driver or honked their horn in annoyance or anger at another driver. I realize it is tempting to react to others that seemingly have driven badly, but doing so can have some really adverse consequences.

Indeed, about 4% of the drivers responding to the survey said that they had actually gotten out of their car to confront another driver, which though this might seem like a small percentage, it translates into potentially 7.6 million drivers that annually get out of their car to go after another driver. There were about 600 gun-involved road rage occurrences in that same year and the number of gun related incidents continues to rise annually. When you add guns into the equation, the deadliness of road rage acts can easily devolve into shootings that lead to severe injuries and even death.

I've seen with my own eyes several road rage incidents that luckily for me, did not directly involve me. You can bet too that I've had my share of bad drivers that have irked me, frustrated me, endangered me, and otherwise could have led to my responding to them. I've pretty much refrained from doing so.

There are some that say that you should respond to those lousy drivers so that they will become more aware about what they've done wrong, presumably trying to alert them and make their roadway guffaw moment into a helpful driving lesson for them. In my experience, this notion that you are somehow going to improve the other driver's driving habits by honking or yelling at them is a wild stretch of the imagination. Another justifying reason sometimes given to react is that by doing so you are warning other drivers, since presumably the nearby drivers can see that you are giving the finger to the other driver or otherwise drawing attention to them. Once again, I doubt that this attempt to possibly put a spotlight on those other drivers is really being done to try and benefit fellow drivers.

Maybe I'm an advocate of passivism in these matters, which I realize some of you might disagree with, but I tend to believe that you are better off to let go of the moment of potential reactive anger, which otherwise could lead to a lifetime of angst, suffering, and regret.

One day, I was driving along in the as-usual sluggish Southern California freeway traffic when I noticed up ahead that two cars were pulled over into the emergency lane. The drivers were outside of their cars and standing between the two now parked automobiles. I could see that they were yelling and pointing feverishly at each other. The situation looked dire. Given the high number of TV shows that are filmed here on our freeways, I actually looked around to see if maybe there was a film crew and these were paid actors. Sadly, it was real life.

Just as I slowly drove past, one took a swing at the other one. I watched in shock and horror in my rear view mirror as they started to duke it out, right there on the freeway, in bold and bright daylight, on what otherwise should have been a sunny and cheerful Monday. A police car was making its way up to the scene and I later read in the news about how the two men beat each other up and the officer had to stop them from likely killing each other.

Road Rage Can Be a Criminal Offense

This case was an obvious one involving criminal behavior. Many people don't realize that road rage can in fact readily be a criminal offense, even if you don't get out of your cars to perform a street performance boxing match. Intentional assault is for most states a criminal act, and if you use your car to try and assault someone, such as trying to ram them or driving them off-the-road, you can be subject to prosecution and potential jail time. Road rage incidents can result in jail or prison incarceration, it can include a driver's license suspension, it can include compulsory anger management classes, and can involve civil lawsuits and financial penalties.

The garden variety type of road rage plays out every day and by-and-large goes unpunished and generally unreported. It can include the average driver that is relatively unknown to the rest of the world and so it is just part and parcel of the daily drive. Or, it can involve big time celebrities. For example, the famous comedian and actor Chevy Chase was recently reported as being involved in a road rage incident in New York. According to the news, the comedian alleged that the other driver cut him off, and so he opted to chase up to catch him, they then both got out of their cars, there was a scuffle, and now there are accusations about who swung at whom first.

We tend to be surprised when we hear that a well-to-do person got involved in road rage. The thinking is that someone that has wealth, fame, prestige, and otherwise societal success, would not allow themselves to be drawn into road rage. Why mess with it? Just shrug it off and move on. I suppose it shows that as humans, we are all susceptible to wanting to defend ourselves. No matter what else we might already have, we are still offended by perceived offenses and have a natural tendency to react.

Another theory is that when we are in our cars, we begin to lose touch with reality. Inside the cocoon of the car, we perceive a certainly amount of safety and autonomy. We are detached from the outside world and it is as though we are actually in a simulator. What is occurring outside the windshield might as well be on a movie screen. We also become emboldened in our cars. We are more apt to yell or give the finger toward someone, in contrast to if you were standing on the street and facing the other person directly. People that might otherwise be shy or reserved will have a tremendous feeling of empowerment, since they perceive they are protected by a ton of metal and steel.

We also at times seem to get into our minds the aspects of what is right and wrong in the world, and as a driver we are watching for those that digress from what we believe to be proper etiquette in driving. If another driver suddenly cuts into your lane and fails to properly signal, for you, that's an offense. For someone else, even if the person signaled, and even if the person waited to get into the lane, the driver being "imposed upon" might perceive that no one should be cutting in front of them. The driving etiquette is highly variable by person and so what might seem like an innocent move to some is a punishable-by-death-sentence offense by another.

I knew one driver that told me that for the empty roadway space in front of his car and up to the next car ahead, he considered that his "personal space" and that any driver that wanted to invade it would need to be worthy. Worthiness to him included the type of car that wanted to breech into the space, how the other car signaled, and other factors. Seems pretty wacky. Well, with over 200 million cars in the United States, and when you consider that just about any adult can pretty much get a driver's license, the mindset of drivers is going to be all over the map. Not all drivers necessarily have in their minds the same rational thoughts as the rest of us.

Besides the overall mindset of drivers, we also need to consider the moment to moment mental mindset of drivers. A very otherwise rational driver might have just gotten fired at work that afternoon, or maybe they had a terrible argument with a loved one. They get into their car, and they are already an internally boiling brew of anger. All it takes is a simple act by another driver, maybe veering a bit close to their car, and it is like the proverbial match that lights a fire. The person that has all this other pent-up anger now lets it spill forth, partially emboldened by being in their car cocoon. This kind of explains why we sometimes see otherwise seemingly caring people that just go nuts with road rage.

Getting caught up in the moment is a key factor involved often in road rage. The other day, I was standing in an elevator, minding my own business, and another person got into the elevator and opted to stand right next to me. This was a big enough elevator that the person could easily have been several feet from me. But, no, the person had to stand within inches of me. My first thought was that the person was rude and I even wondered whether they had some other ulterior motive in mind. Why invade my private space? I decided to go ahead and move to the other side of the elevator, wanting to see whether the other person would say anything or do anything. They did not. In this case, probably it was just that the person was unaware of their transgression. Or, at least, in my view, their perceived transgression.

The same can happen when we are driving our cars. Another driver makes a move, it might be something that seems like a transgression, but to them maybe it is not. They might be blissfully unaware of their actions. It could be that the driver is just someone that doesn't pay attention to others on the roadways. Or, maybe it's the driver that just got fired and so they are driving more aggressively than normal, but don't realize they are doing so. All in all, the point is that the in-the-moment factor is often what makes or breaks a road rage incident. It would seem rarer that there are those that are road rage "professionals" that seek out acts of committing road rage. It does happen, for sure, but the preponderance of road rage is more akin to moments of perceived transgressions.

Police will generally tell you that chasing after another car when you believe that you've been acted upon by a road rage perpetrator is not a good idea and indeed you should not take such action (get the license plate number and call 911 instead). By chasing after another car, you are endangering all other cars and drivers, along with pedestrians, and so you are making a bad situation even worse. The millions of daily road rage incidents are pretty much defused because there is no cascading reaction involved. It's when the road rage incident is escalated and becomes a series of larger and larger steps that it gets out-of-hand. The two drivers that I mentioned had stopped on the freeway in the emergency lane had indeed escalated whatever was occurring. They were also endangering the other drivers by putting on the spectacle. Other drivers could have inadvertently rammed into each other by the distraction, and likewise being in the emergency lane meant that it could not be used easily for a true emergency, etc. These road rage engulfed drivers didn't likely think about that aspect, and were only thinking about themselves.

There are some that say you should show remorse to another driver that has committed some kind of initiating road rage act. If someone else cuts you off while you are driving, you are to show them love instead of hate. Be the bigger person. I suppose this is quite admirable, but I think it is not only hard to bring yourself to take this stance, but it can also be perceived by the road rage instigator as an act of offense. The instigator might further escalate the road rage due to your act of love. The same is somewhat true if you are the instigator. If another car honks at you, and you control yourself and opt to say thanks instead of getting angry, it can actually set the other person into a rage. For me, the taking of almost any reactive action is bound to more likely escalate the matter, rather than diffuse it (of course, each particular instance and circumstances dictate this).

A simple model of the road rage behavior consists of an instigator that performs some act, and a reactor that responds to the act.

We've got this: Instigator -> Reactor

If all goes generally well, the matter ends with the reactor and there's no escalation involved, and hopefully the instigating act did not cause any direct harm to begin with, other than maybe a close call.

Due to the potential for escalation, it can become this: Instigator -> Reactor -> Instigator

Here, the instigator led to the reactor, which led to the reactor reacting, which now has promoted the instigator to take further action. Hopefully, things come to a stop and this doesn't get more pronounced.

But, it can go further: Instigator -> Reactor -> Instigator -> Reactor .... {repeat}

What can happen is that the process escalates, with repeated acts upon the instigator and the reactor, often getting larger and larger. This can continue until unfortunately they end-up injuring or maybe even killing each other. The escalation or chain reaction can occur over many minutes or it can occur quickly as in just a matter of seconds.

All it takes is for a car going 80 miles per hour to affront another driver, which that driver then tries to ram the first driver, and they both hit each other and cause a car wreck. It can play out with the blink of an eye. Other situations like the two drivers that got into the emergency lane and fought each other by-hand, had probably taken maybe ten to fifteen minutes to first get entangled and then pull over and get out of their cars.

Road Rage and Personality Types

Some research suggests that the action and reactions are also tied to the personality types of the persons involved. A type A aggressive personality will possibly take a different action than say a type B moderate personality. We can assign the personality types to the instigator and the reactor, and see how that plays out.

Suppose:

Instigator: Type A aggressive personality

Reactor: Type B moderate personality

Fast end: Instigator of Type A -> Reactor of Type B

Depending upon the situation, the road rage potentially stops before it gets extended. The Type B personality shrugs off the incident and does not escalate.

Suppose instead it is this: Instigator Type A -> Reactor Type A.

It is believed that this will be an increased odds of an escalation, in that the reactor being a type A will be more likely to react and then this will lead to the instigator type A further responding, and so on.

We then have these four combinations:

Fast end: Instigator Type A -> Reactor Type B

Extensive escalation: Instigator Type A -> Reactor Type A

Mild escalation: Instigator Type B -> Reactor Type A

Quickest end: Type B -> Reactor Type B

One issue though about these personality types studies involves the situation or circumstance involved. Even a type B personality might escalate if it just so happened that morning that they had gotten fired from their job or otherwise are in a highly emotional state. A type A might be mellow on a particular day and circumstance. Also, the nature of the instigating act can be a significant determiner. The personality types offer an overall indication of what might happen, but it is contextual based as to how things will actually unfold.

When considering the outcome of a road rage, there is a range of outcomes that can occur, including:

- No harm, no foul (relatively instantaneous and then forgotten)

- Psychological harm (momentary versus long lasting)

- Physical harm (car-to-car, via gun, via other attack)

- Other

One interesting aspect is that a mild road rage act can plant the seed for a future more overt road rage act. Let's suppose a car cuts me off. I am irked and at the moment and do nothing. But, this boils up in me. Twenty minutes later, a completely different car cuts me off. That's it, I scream and exclaim to the world that I've had it with these instigators. So, I vent and proceed to go after this particular driver. It could be that maybe this driver made a simple mistake and was unknowingly cutting me off, but at this point I have in my mind that I have been offended enough by these acts that I finally decide to take action. I allow the accumulation of all those other offensive drivers to now become my act of revenge.

In that sense, the road rage acts are like a virus. Each instance can infect each other driver. Some drivers will be able to just shrug it off and it won't have any lasting effect. Others will add it to the pile of such offenses. Eventually, a tipping point is reached. The last straw falls on the camel's back. And therefore someone that otherwise would not have likely been a road rage active participant, now decides to rid the earth of these road rage idiots. If this happens with the wrong kind of instigator, you get yourself the road rage exponential impact.

Speaking of instigators, we need to consider what motivates them. It could be that an instigator has performed an act completely by innocence. They didn't realize that what they did would be offensive to another driver. Or, they didn't see that the other driver was there. Etc. Or, it could be that the instigator knew that did something untoward, but they view it as the normal course of driving. Driving is a shark's game, they believe, and we all need to grab for whatever territory we can. They might have intentionally started the road rage because they like to be a troublemaker and want to see what will happen. There are a seemingly endless number of intentions.

Reactors have similar kinds of mindsets. There are some reactors that will make a mountain out of a mole hill, in that if another car even dares to seemingly do the tiniest offensive act, they will react. Others have a high tolerance and either don't notice offensive acts, or figure offensive acts are just part of the driving game, and so on.

It can also be confusing at times as to who is an instigator versus a reactor, and also how someone can get tossed into this dangerous roadway game. I've seen the case of a misidentified instigator as prodded by a misguided reactor — allow me to explain.

There was a black sedan ahead of me that cut-off a sports car, the black sedan zoomed ahead into a bunch of gnarly traffic, the sports car that was cut-off tried to catch-up, and then mistakenly seemed to think that a different black sedan that had nothing to do with any of this was the original instigator. I saw the sports car get right behind the misidentified black sedan, and then the sports car turned its headlights on-and-off and put on its brights, presumably trying to show displeasure to what he thought was the instigator. Chock this up to a misguided reactor going after a misidentified instigator.

Of course, as you might guess, this sadly drew the misidentified black sedan into the situation and now it wanted to react to the sports car. And so the ball gets rolling, sickeningly. Proof that two wrongs don't make a right.

There's also the instigator that seems out for blood, for no apparent reason, for anyone that might be on the roadway. Usually, a road rage of one instigator will irk one reactor, and they then start a chain reaction that includes themselves and possibly spills over to other drivers. But, I've also seen a driver that cuts off car-after-car, weaving in and out of traffic, and leaves in their wake a platoon of reactors. Is the instigator drunk and just driving erratically? Or, is the driver a nut that is determined to wreak havoc upon the world? Sometimes it's one, sometimes it's the other.

You've got your drunk drivers, your careless drivers, your partying drivers, your pushy drivers, your rushed drivers, your tailgating drivers, your speeding drivers, your cut-off drivers, your honking drivers, your turn-signal irritating drivers, and on and on. There are some drivers that drive an expensive car and so they think they should have the right way of the road. There are some drivers that resent drivers that have an expensive car and so they want to show them that the rest of us with inexpensive cars won't be pushed around.

Pretty much, when you are driving, you have the entire mixture of society and culture that will dictate how people will drive. You cannot somehow extract out of the equation the human elements of how they perceive the world, what their beliefs are, how they handle their emotions, what their life status is, and the rest. It's all immersed into the driving act and being on the roadways.

What does this have to do with AI self-driving cars?

At the Cybernetic Self-Driving Car Institute, we are developing AI self-driving cars that can deal with road rage.

Now, there are some pundits of AI self-driving cars that will tell you that there will never be any road rage once we have self-driving cars. In their utopian world, the AI of the self-driving cars will determine how all cars on the roadways act and react, and so the human elements of road rage are expunged from the equation. Road rage solved. It will never ever occur again.

Hogwash!

Let's consider the first aspect which is an assumption that all cars will magically overnight be AI self-driving cars. Instead, the adoption of AI self-driving cars is going to happen over a lengthy time and that we will for many, many years have a mixture of both conventional human-driven cars and AI self-driving cars. This means that for decades we will have humans driving and automation driving.

There will be human drivers that will still be experiencing road rage at other human drivers. This stays the same as with our world today. Some say it might get even worse, since the road rage against AI self-driving cars won't exist as much, and so the volume of road rage will be enacted upon an increasingly smaller set of human driven cars. The per capita road rage might increase, some predict.

There will also though be human drivers that will experience road rage against AI self-driving cars. Make no mistake about that.

Human drivers are going to get upset at AI self-driving cars. You might say that's stupid of those humans to so react, but I assure they will get upset at self-driving cars. Whether the self-driving car intended to cut someone off or otherwise did something amiss in the mind of the human driver, it really won't matter that the AI presumably was innocent, the human is going to get upset anyway at the perceived affront.

The human driver will then potentially try to ram the self-driving car, or force it off the road, or shoot at the human passengers inside, etc. In essence, all of the same reactions that the human driver might have toward another human driver can readily play out by the human driver toward an AI self-driving car.

Since that's the case, what do we want our AI self-driving cars to do?

From an ethics perspective, you might say that the AI should not react to the instigator, but that's a somewhat shortsighted view. If another car is trying to ram an AI self-driving car, are you suggesting that the AI self-driving car should let this happen? I think not. The AI self-driving car would likely need to take evasive action, which I would think we all would agree is prudent. If there are human occupants inside the AI self-driving car, you can pretty much bet that they certainly want the AI to try and protect them.

OK, so now I assume you are on-board with the idea that the AI self-driving car is going to get involved in road rages, presumably as a reactor rather than as an instigator.

Well, I'd like to gently point out that the role of the instigator can be in the mind of the beholder.

If an AI self-driving car comes up to a four-way stop, and it moves ahead before a human driven car that also came to the stop, and even if the self-driving car had the right-of-way, the human driver might believe that the AI instigated a road rage because it slighted them. Or, if that's not enough for you, suppose a self-driving car is on the freeway and needs to take an emergency action because there is debris on the roadway, so it rapidly switches lanes and slightly cuts off another driver. Maybe that other driver, a human, did not see the debris and so has no idea why the AI cut them off. Or, maybe the other driver saw the debris but felt that the AI should have taken the lane to the left instead of the lane to the right that they are in. And so on. The human might react to the "instigator" act of the AI self-driving car.

Innocent AI Self-Driving Car Can Still Get Into Road Rage

There's another angle here too. Suppose an AI self-driving car is not doing anything untoward at all. It pulls up to an intersection. A human driven car also pulls up to the intersection and is sitting right next to the AI self-driving car. The human occupants in the self-driving car opt to roll down the windows. They yell and taunt the humans in the other car. Maybe they even point a gun at the other car. The human driven car now perceives this as an instigation and so the human driver tries to ram the self-driving car.

Voila, we now have another example of an AI self-driving car being involved in a road rage incident. You might complain and say that it's not fair to blame the AI self-driving car in this last case, since it is the unruly humans inside the AI self-driving car that led to the altercation. Yes, that's true, but notice that the point is that it involves an AI self-driving car. Thus, the utopian view that says there won't be any more road rages is a mistaken view, even if we were to have all self-driving cars.

Now, if we did magically have only AI self-driving cars on the roadways, at least (in theory), we could limit the road rage acts to being done without the intended effort by the self-driving car itself. For example, we have two AI self-driving cars come up to an intersection. They are side-by-side. Both cars have human occupants. The human occupants roll down their windows and shout at each other, and then start shooting guns at each other. The AI itself presumably won't try to ram the other car, and nor will the AI of the other car try to ram the first car.

This though raises another thorny topic. To what degree will we allow the human occupants to get the AI to take certain kinds of driving actions? Suppose I'm in an AI self-driving car, and the AI self-driving car next to me has human occupants that point a gun at me. I want my AI self-driving car to speed away. I don't want to sit there like a sitting duck. I am assuming most of you would agree with me that the AI should be able to react or act upon instructions if the human occupants have some kind of emergency.

How far though can this AI reaction go? If I ask my self-driving car to speed ahead, and suppose it's a red light, should the AI allow my self-driving car to violate the law and go through the red light? And if so, how might it endanger other cars and other human occupants? Here's a real mind bender – suppose I ask my self-driving car to ram the other car, in order to presumably stop it from harming me, a human occupant in the AI self-driving car? This might a prudent solution to the problem at hand, and you can't completely rule out that this would never ever be permitted.

For humans, when they are driving, we often see humans that are like a Dr. Jekyll and Mr. Hyde, in that they suddenly snap and become ferocious drivers or react emotionally to what is happening on the roadways. A professional bodyguard driver knows that sometimes ramming another car might be the proper and prudent means to stop a bad situation from getting worse or forcing it off the road. This a perfectly rational act and not necessarily one that was motivated by emotion. Will we expect our AI self-driving cars to do the same?

Those that have a utopian view believe that an AI self-driving car should never do anything that would harm or impinge on other cars. This is a naïve view of the world. Those other cars, even when driven by AI, might have humans in them that have dastardly acts in mind and want to carry them out. Unless we are going to make AI self-driving cars into vaults, such that when humans get into them there is nothing else they can do, other than be essentially imprisoned within them, we need to assume that the human element is still going to come to play on our roadways.

We need to have highly sophisticated AI that can be aware of how to take evasive actions and be able to respond to road rage. The AI needs to be able to interact with the human occupants of the self-driving car, and be able to ascertain whether any commands given by the humans should be carried out or not.

If we are going to ask that we have self-driving cars, we need to also realize the importance of the driving task and that it involves more than simply driving down a highway. Since we are saying that we want self-driving cars that can drive like humans, it means that the AI also needs to be able to know how to properly take defensive actions, and even actions considered of a more proactive nature, as dependent upon the circumstances.

This brings up another facet of the AI of self-driving cars. A chunk of the AI savviness is based on artificial neural networks which are looking for patterns in driving behaviors. When training the neural network, we use lots of driving situations and feed those into the neural network to do pattern matching. Suppose that the dataset has instances of road rage – what will the neural network "learn" from those instances? If there are too few, it could be that the system lands on a pattern of response that we would not want undertaken. Without some form of guidance or supervision to that learning, we could have the AI reacting in an oddball manner, perhaps reacting incorrectly to a true road rage, or acting incorrectly to a situation that is not actually a road rage.

The AI needs to be on the lookout for potential road rage circumstances and be using the sensory data to try and do an early detection of such a situation. During the sensor fusion and updates to the internal virtual model of the surrounding driving world, the AI should be finding telltale clues. If a road rage appears imminent, we would want the AI to have the self-driving car take a defensive posture, hopefully avoiding the road rage. This could be road rage that is aimed at the self-driving car, or it could be road rage aimed at other nearby cars and for which the self-driving car wants to avoid getting entangled into it.

With the gradual advent of V2V, vehicle-to-vehicle communications, there is also the potential for one AI of a self-driving car to alert other nearby AI's of other self-driving cars about a possible road rage emerging. This then would provide a helpful heads-up for those other self-driving cars. In a more involved fashion, the self-driving cars could even act together to try and defuse the road rage, thus, rather than each individual self-driving car backing away, perhaps they strategically work as a momentary virtual team of self-driving cars to minimize the road rage act.

One advantage of self-driving cars will be that they will nearly all be outfitted with video cameras and other sensory devices that can record what is happening on the roadways. This is an advantage due to the aspect that often when a road rage occurs today, it becomes a he-said she-said situation. One driver claims that another driver cut them off. The other driver refutes the allegation. It's hard to know what really did happen. Sometimes other drivers will come forward to say what they saw. But, those other drivers might be unreliable or have a grudge or otherwise might even innocently misreport what occurred. With self-driving cars, the odds are that we'll have not only the recorded evidence that's in the involved self-driving cars, but we could potentially collect similar recorded evidence from other nearby self-driving cars that were witnesses to the incident.

For some of us, this seems like a great thing, for others it might be seen as a bit scary and somewhat Big Brother like.

In any case, as I've tried to indicate, road rage is not going away. Unless society as a whole has a brainwashing and we can get people to be always and entirely be civil toward one another, we're going to continue to have road rage. It will happen while there is a mixture of both human driven cars and AI self-driving cars. And, as I've mentioned, it will even continue when we reach the utopian world of all self-driving cars.

For many of the auto makers and tech firms that are developing AI self-driving cars, they are focusing right now on just getting the AI to be able to drive the car. After we get the AI self-driving car version 1.0 nailed down, we'll need to be moving toward version 2.0. That's where the road rage handling capabilities will be considered not just as an add-on, but an essential component of a true AI self-driving car.

CHAPTER 10
CONSPIRACY THEORIES
AND
SELF-DRIVING CARS

CHAPTER 10

CONSPIRACY THEORIES
AND
SELF-DRIVING CARS

What do these aspects have in common: Roswell, Area 51, JFK assassination, moon landing, AI self-driving cars?

They are all considered by some to be conspiracies.

Most of us are familiar with Roswell, New Mexico and the claims of a UFO that landed there. Likewise, most of us know about the claimed mysteries of Area 51. The JFK assassination, even after all these years and multiple investigations, still raises the question about who was on the grassy knoll and how was JFK actually shot. Could Lee Harvey Oswald have really been able to get all those shots off, in the short amount of time, and hit his target with such precision? Some would say, no way.

For the moon landing, you might only be vaguely aware that there are some that believe it never actually happened. It was presumably faked. Indeed, here in Southern California, on one of our many Hollywood studio lots, it is believed that there was a sound stage that was made into a lunar landscape. What you see in the live broadcast of us landing on the moon was actually taking place on a large set and the astronauts were really here on Earth. Some claim that we never got into space at all. Others concede that we did get into outer space, but that we had intractable problems and could not get to the moon. Thus, in order to save face within the United States and with the entire world, an elaborate ruse was put together.

So, do you think we landed on the moon?

If so, those that believe in the conspiracy theory would say that you are naïve. You have allowed the government to trick you. You are a rube.

That being said, the last item in the conspiracies list might catch you by surprise.

AI self-driving cars.

Yes, there's a conspiracy story going around about AI self-driving cars. It's not reached the "big time" like Roswell or JFK, but it's definitely something that is being whispered and wondered about. In fact, when I give presentations about self-driving cars, one of the questions I invariably get asked is whether or not there is indeed a conspiracy underlying the emergence of AI self-driving cars.

Admittedly, the first time that I got asked the question it was a bit disarming and I almost thought it was an April Fool's joke. Say, what? A conspiracy about AI self-driving cars? What do you mean, I asked the person that offered the question.

Let's back-up a moment and first review the nature of conspiracy theories.

Typically, a conspiracy theory involves a belief that there is some form of secret plot that has untoward intentions and involves multiple conspirators that concoct and try to carry out their evil doing. Furthermore, there is usually a tangled web that makes it hard for outsiders to figure out the true nature and structure of the conspirators. The conspiracy can possibly exist for quite a while before it is discovered. Even once it is discovered, the ability to ferret out the full underpinnings is often quite difficult and it is so well hidden and camouflaged that one might not ever get to the bottom of it.

I'll add possibly a new word to your vocabulary, dietrologia. This is a word that entails the belief that any official explanation for something is unlikely to be the real explanation, and there's something else really going on. Those that embrace a conspiracy theory are apt to have a tendency toward dietrologia. Whenever shown a set of facts or told a story, they are right away skeptical and assume that there is an unstated and purposely hidden reality underneath that needs to be discovered.

Of course, there's a chance that sometimes they'll be right. You might say that Watergate was an example of a true conspiracy. It involved higher ups. It involved subterfuge. It was hidden. It took a while to figure out. There were conspirators. It was done for an untoward reason. It had disbelievers at first. Those that thought it was a conspiracy were at first accused of being paranoid and making things up. And so on.

Thus, we do need to agree that there are real conspiracies and there are imaginary ones. Just because someone spouts out about a conspiracy does not suggest that they are delusion or crazed. We need to give a moment of reflection about whether the conspiracy might be real. This can be hard to do, in the sense that the conspiracy might seem so ridiculous, so out-of-touch, so imaginative, we could be tempted to provide a knee jerk response that it's just a bunch of baloney.

There are some conspiracies that are shallow, and others that are deep. The shallow ones are usually easier to spot and figure out. The deep ones will often have a wide array of tentacles and once you find one part of the octopus, you later discover there's another arm or leg that you didn't realize existed. Inevitably, you begin to wonder how deep it will go. Is there any end to it at all? Maybe it involves everyone.

Some key principles underlying the basis for conspiracies includes:

- Nothing happens by accident

- Nothing is as it seems

- Everything is connected

Could it be that Lee Harvey Oswald just so happened on his own to decide to kill JFK and was able to pull off a seemingly impossible task? It's hard to believe that this happened by the efforts of a solitary individual. Some believe that the industrial military complex was worried about JFK and whether he would support our defense spending. Some believe that the communists were worried about JFK. Somehow, all of these stakeholders plotted to assassinate JFK.

Enemies All Around Us

Conspiracies also play on the notion that there are enemies all around us. In fact, you are supposed to be considering these kinds of enemies:

- Enemies outside

- Enemies within

- Enemies above

- Enemies below

One consideration too is why a conspiracy would take place. When you think about it, you'd realize that pulling off a conspiracy could take a lot of work. Experts that have examined the moon landing have claimed that there were about 411,000 people that were involved in getting to the moon. If that's the case, imagine trying to get that many people to keep a lid on the conspiracy. Seems almost impossible. Experts claim that at the normally predicted rate that people tend to divulge secrets, it would have taken around 3 ½ years to ultimately have the whole thing become publicly known and unravel.

I realize that my definition of a conspiracy indicated that the effort is being done for an untoward reason. Some argue that you can have a conspiracy that's being done for the sake of goodness. Suppose the United Nations undertook a secret project to create a vaccine that could eradicate a devastating disease that's found in developing countries. It's possible then that a conspiracy could be undertaken for beneficial reasons. Most though would say that conspiracies are nearly always for untoward reasons. There are powerful actors that want to ruin other people's lives. The conspiracy exists to harm people and it is inevitably a battle of light versus darkness, or of good versus evil.

Conspiracy investigators say that the first way to discover what's going on involves asking the simple question of "who benefits?" and that then you can begin to find clues to the puzzle. Does the government benefit? Does private enterprise benefit? Who will reap the benefits of the conspiracy? For Watergate, we now know that President Nixon was intended to benefit, along with his administration, and presumably his supporters.

Having true conspiracies is especially handy for those that believe in imaginary ones. If all conspiracies were shown to be untrue, it would make things very hard to float any new conspiracies. Anyone could refute the new conspiracy by quickly pointing out that none of the prior ones held water. Fortunately for the conspiracy theorists, by having some bona fide examples, it provides a glimmer of hope that maybe, just maybe, the new one could also be true.

The twist to conspiracies is that they are usually very hard to disprove.

If you find a person that says a particular conspiracy is false, I might insist that the person is lying. They are actually part of the conspiracy. They were told to lie about it. For whatever you come up with to try and undermine the conspiracy, I can just try to absorb your contention into the conspiracy itself. I'll just keep making the conspiracy bigger and bigger. For Roswell, the local police say there's no space alien that was there. Aha, the police are part of the conspiracy. For Roswell, the military says there's no space alien. Obviously the military must be part of the conspiracy. The president of the United States says that there isn't a space alien here. This means that the president is part of the conspiracy.

Or, another angle is to say that those that refute the conspiracy are blind to it. The president might not be part of the conspiracy, and instead he's just living in a bubble and doesn't know that it is actually true. Maybe the police are being tricked into thinking that the space alien that they saw was something created by the CIA. By and large, conspiracies are so malleable that you can just keep morphing it so that any resisters are either part of the conspiracy or they are oblivious to its existence.

Let's now turn our attention to AI self-driving cars.

At the Cybernetic Self-Driving Car Institute, we are developing AI systems for self-driving cars. I genuinely believe that we are doing so for beneficial purposes of humanity. Along the way, we are also hopefully going to be appropriately compensated for bringing to society something that will aid us all.

Just to let you know, there are conspiracy theorists that would say we are either blind to the true AI self-driving car conspiracy, or we are naïve about its existence.

I leave it to you to judge.

The AI Self-Driving Car Conspiracy Explained

So, what exactly is the AI self-driving car conspiracy?

The most prevalent version indicates that the advent of AI self-driving cars is being done for evil purposes to harm humanity. It is being undertaken by powerful conspirators that are purposely seeking to subjugate humans to AI. First, AI will take over our cars. We will lose the ability to drive a car. We will become dependent upon AI for our mobility. We won't be able to get around without the use of the AI. Once this happens, the AI will grow from there. Step by step, AI will ultimately become sentient and we humans will become its slave.

By seemingly innocently using AI for cars, the unwashed of us are letting AI into our daily lives. If we knew the true full plot, we'd be resisting at every turn. But, because it seems plausible that having AI for self-driving cars is a good idea, we are opening the door or the window to this AI. And, in the proverbial give an inch, take a mile, the whole thing is secretive and incremental. We will soon discover that

AI have taken over our entire existence, and we allowed it to happen by sneakily letting it occur via our cars.

Who benefits?

The tech firms would presumably love to subjugate us all to technology. They adore technology more than they like people, or so we are led to believe.

Or, it could be that the auto makers are doing this, since they not only want us to buy their cars, they'd love to control where we go and what we do, presumably.

Maybe it's the government. What better way to go toward Big Brother. Get us to use AI self-driving cars, and the next thing you know, they are controlling our minds.

Some would say it's the AI community in particular. Many AI developers were earlier the butt of jokes as to not being able to produce intelligent automated systems. They got so upset that they decided they'd show us what can be done. It's a pride thing.

It could be an overarching evil cabal. The tech firms are in cahoots with the auto firms, which are in cahoots with the AI community, which are in cahoots with the government. This is the grand conspiracy. All of these powerful actors are co-conspirators. They have plotted together for their evil doing.

Are you skeptical?

Of course you would be. You are part of the brainwashed herd. You can't grasp the aspect that these powerful actors would want to undertake such an effort.

Why have AI self-driving cars so suddenly become of interest? Do you naïve believe it just happened by accident? That's pretty foolish on your part.

Why are the government regulators being so easy on AI self-driving cars? Do you really think they would resist trying to regulate heavily these potential death machines? Obviously, they are in on it. They don't care that some people will get injured or killed during the course of perfecting the AI self-driving car. That's a small price to pay for getting ultimately to Big Brother.

Even the media seems to be part of the conspiracy. Only lately have there been any kind of media skepticism about self-driving cars. Up until now, it's all been rosy. The media is either part of the conspiracy, or so out-of-touch that it does not see a conspiracy when it sits right in front of their noses.

Let's try to disprove this particular conspiracy or prove it.

How could the auto firms, the tech firms, the AI community, the government, have all banded together to plan and carry out the conspiracy? Doesn't seem plausible.

Now, that being said, I don't have anyone that can come forward and say they were part of the conspiracy and reveal its inner workings. Is there anyone probing these entities to find out what secretive memos they might have? We don't know.

It seems we can neither disprove it, and nor can we prove it.

Well, here's an idea.

The industrial military complex, which pulled off the JFK assassination, they got together with the CIA that has kept Roswell a secret, and banded with the team that did the fake moon landing, and have come back together for purposes of bringing forth AI self-driving cars.

This conspiracy includes them, along with the AI developers, the auto firms, the tech companies, the government, the police, and the space aliens. Yes, even the space aliens are part of it (they are going to seed the AI self-driving cars with a back-door that will allow them to take over humanity – it's like the movie Inception, a conspiracy within a conspiracy within a conspiracy).

I'm sure of it.

Or, am I just saying so to keep the real conspiracy from your keen eyes?

CHAPTER 11

FEAR LANDSCAPE

AND

SELF-DRIVING CARS

CHAPTER 11

FEAR LANDSCAPE
AND SELF-DRIVING CARS

Fear is considered one of the foundational elements of emotion.

It seems as though humans and pretty much all animals are prone to fear. Fear can be based on a real situation, such as you might be standing in front of a hungry lion and so you naturally are bound to be fearful of it, or fear might be based on a perceived danger that is not necessarily directly evident, such as walking down a dark alley and being inherently suspicious that something bad might happen to you.

Typically, there is a physical response in a human or animal when experiencing fear. You have likely been on a roller coaster and in anticipation of that big drop up ahead your heart rate goes up, you feel your body tensing, your mind might become laser focused and you can't think of anything other than the circumstance that you are facing. Humans have an ability to detect fear on others, including via facial expression analysis (someone's face gets tense), the person might clench their teeth and make fists with their hands, etc. Of course, animals can also detect fear, of which I'm guessing you've had cases whereby a dog sensed your fear, maybe smelling your perspiration, and either took advantage of your fearful state or in some instances maybe even tried to reduce it.

Responding to fear can be as simple as the classic fight-or-flight kind of response. If you fear something, you might decide to stand your ground and fight it. Alternatively, you might instead decide to run from whatever is causing the fear. Regrettably, sometimes while in the grip of fear we make bad choices. It could be that you should have chosen to run away from an angry bear rather than trying to confront it. Maybe trying to run away from an approaching ball of fire would have been better handled by trying to shelter in place.

There are other options beyond just fight-or-flight, including one that can be the worse of them all, freezing up. Sometimes the fear is so overwhelming that trying to ascertain what to do is beyond our mental capacity at the moment, and thus we become frozen in fear. Though it might be possible that being frozen will work out okay in the given situation, generally some response is more likely to be successful than no response at all.

Another twist to fear is that it can be considered plausible or implausible (some would say valid or invalid).

The other day there was a Chinese space station that was going to fall to earth and supposedly no one could predict where it would ultimately land. I had a colleague that told me he was fearful it could land on him. I tried to point out that the vast majority of the globe is water and so the odds were high that it would fall into the water and not strike anyone in particular. Even if it fell over land, I pointed out that by being inside a structure such as a building, it would seem unlikely he'd get hit and killed. The odds that he would be outside and be struck by it were likely much less odds than say winning the multi-state lotto (I realize he'd rather win the lotto than get hit by the space station). I suggested he buy the multi-state lotto ticket, the payout was around $500 million, and that maybe he'd win the lotto and get hit by the space station at the same time (those are some amazing odds!).

Anyway, sometimes fear is in our minds, but not due to an actual fearful situation per se. We can convince ourselves to be fearful. In that sense, fear is definitely a dual-edged sword. Fear provides us with a vital survival technique. When utilized poorly, it can cause us to damage ourselves as based on a false believe that something dangerous is going to happen, when let's say there's really no chance of it happening at all. Some would refer to this as an unfounded fear.

A fascinating recent study examined fear and described an angle that most would not have thought of. We all know that you are bound to be fearful of a predator. The field mouse is fearful of the swooping hawk. The prey is fearful of the predator, and rightfully so. This particular study pointed out that animals tend to avoid eating feces or munching on a carcass that has gone bad. Those aren't predators, so why fear them? It's because we are fearful of getting infections or disease, and seem to realize that we need to avoid circumstances that might involve getting infected by some untoward bacteria.

How do animals know about this? In the nature-versus-nurture debate, are we programmed in our DNA to avoid things that might infect us, or do we only learn over time by either watching others, or by being taught, or by getting an infection and surviving it such that we realize not to do that again? If you see a hawk diving at you, it's a pretty obvious aspect that maybe you should avoid letting it get you. But, seeing a juicy carcass, when you are starving, and opting to avoid eating it, because you somehow know that hours or maybe days later you might get sick, and might die, now that's an interesting aspect of fear. You need to connect a later-on consequence to something that at the moment seems benign.

The researchers described a landscape of fear. Animals will avoid drinking contaminated water. Animals will avoid eating a carcass when it seems too far gone. Animals will even graze away from an area that had a carcass, as though realizing that whatever is bad about the carcass could be spread locally beyond just the carcass. Animals tend to flee from biting ticks or try to get the ticks off their bodies. Within the landscape of fear, animals are able to detect infection threats. Either instinctively or in a learned manner, animals weigh the risks associated with the threats and try to achieve various levels of safety. For any of you interested in population dynamics and ecological aspects, you'd likely find this view of predator avoidance and infection avoidance of keen fascination.

What does this have to do with AI self-driving cars?

At the Cybernetic Self-Driving Car Institute, we are developing an aspect of AI systems for self-driving cars that involves leveraging a landscape of fear regarding driving cars. Allow me a moment to elaborate.

As a human driver, you presumably already have a fear of hitting another car. You likely are fearful that you might hit a pedestrian. You probably also have a fear that other drivers are going to hit your car. You might have a fear that your car will fail on you, such as being on the freeway and all of a sudden it conks out and you are stranded in the middle of the busy freeway in a stalled car. It is possible you have a fear that the roadway will be unusable or unpassable. The other day I drove up to the local mountains and reached a point that the paved road turned to packed dirt, which then became loose dirt, which then became mud due to recent rains. My car almost got stuck in the middle-of-nowhere in an unpassable road (I was driving just a conventional car and not an off-the-road vehicle).

All of the above fears as a human driver are plausible. They are founded on a reasonable belief that those things could happen. We daily harness those fears while driving our cars. Some drivers though make driving mistakes as based on a fear that is either unfounded or at least that doesn't actually materialize.

I was in a car one day with a young driver that notably never made a left turn. He seemed to avoid to the extreme making a left turn. Now, we all know that left turns can be dangerous, and even some of the shipping companies such as UPS are using GPS systems that try to minimize the number of left turns. But, this was left turn paranoia. In talking with the driver, he shared with me a sad story of his family having gotten into a car crash while making a left turn, so he vowed that it would never happen again, which he figured by not making left turns would pretty much guarantee it. I did not have the heart to point out that his now heightened frequency of right turns, being done to make-up for not making left turns, might well have balanced out the risks of making a lesser number of left turns.

His fear of left turns would not have been apparent or visible unless you were observing him, as I had, while a passenger in the car. If you had asked him about his driving approach, I doubt he would have volunteered that he won't make left turns. An outside observer might not have noticed it either, unless you were following him like a secret agent. Our fears then can be hidden from view.

Likewise, when I mentioned that you are fearful of getting into a car crash and fearful of your car faltering, it's not something that you probably would have voiced if I had asked you about it. The word "fear" in our society has various connotations, generally being less flattering to the person that embodies the fear. What, you were fearful of riding that roller coaster, you're a chicken! Society seems to pressure us to hide our fears and tend to not admit to them.

For AI purposes, some believe that if we are to achieve true AI, and be able to make computer systems that can do what humans do, we need to replicate as much as possible whatever humans do. If humans rely on emotions, we must then incorporate emotions into computer systems to achieve true AI. There is a counter-argument that maybe we don't need emotions to have intelligence, and so we can strip away some aspects of humans and yet still arrive at fully intelligent systems. Others say that our intelligence is intertwined with our emotions and you cannot separate them out and yet still have intelligence. Having a no emotions AI system would not end-up being fully intelligent as it has lost an essential component that is wrapped inextricably into intelligence, they would assert.

Whether you stand on one side or the other of the debate about emotion and intelligence, I think we could say that fear is something that does make sense for an intelligent being to possess. If you are willing to consider fear as a form of mathematical calculation about the perceived dangers and risks, we certainly should have that same kind of capability built into our AI systems.

As such, an AI self-driving car should make use of fear. That being said, I am not talking about the kind of "the sky is falling" kind of fear. I am referring to the notion of fear as a methodical means to try and determine risks and dangers, and seek actions to reduce those risks and try to achieve greater chances of safety.

I was in a car with a colleague that likes expensive cars and loves to drive fast (I would say recklessly, while he would say just fast). We were on the freeway in the leftmost lane, the fast lane. Our exit to get off the freeway was fast approaching. He gunned his engine and at the last moment darted across all of the lanes of traffic, having lined up small gaps in each lane, including darting in front of a very large truck hauling a tanker of gasoline. Did we make it to the exit ramp? Yes. Did we hit any cars or trucks? No. In my mind, I was quite fearful when I realized what he was going to try and do. He said that he had no fear because he had done this action many times and he "knew" that he could pull this one off.

For an AI self-driving car, suppose it found itself in a similar situation. You might argue with me that the self-driving car would have been better prepared and would have gradually made its way over to the exit and not needed to leap toward it. But, suppose I told you that the occupant in the self-driving car had suddenly told the self-driving car that they wanted it to make that next exit. Thus, the self-driving car had little time to take the more gradual path to get to the exit.

You could say that the AI should have refused to make the exit. The AI should have said that the occupant had been late in asking and so it was tough luck, and that instead the AI would route the self-driving car to the next exit and then would via side streets make its way back to where that earlier exit had been.

This brings up an important aspect about AI self-driving cars, namely, what is the nature of the driving approach that we want our self-driving cars to have? You might want the AI to do exactly what the "reckless" human driver had done, and have gone for it in terms of making a last gasp dive to the freeway exit. Why is the gradual approach better than the dive for it approach? You might assert that the gradual approach is certainly safer. By what proof do you claim this?

In fact, those that believe we will have a utopian world of all self-driving cars, which I've pointed out is unlikely and that at least for many decades we will have a mix of both human driven cars and self-driving cars, but if we do have all self-driving cars then presumably the dive to the exit would be as safe as any other maneuver. The self-driving car that wanted to dive to the exit could alert all the other self-driving cars nearby, via V2V (vehicle-to-vehicle communications), and the pathway that otherwise randomly had formed for the human driver might now become a designed path instead (based on the cooperation of the other self-driving cars).

We could end-up with extremely aggressive AI self-driving cars. It all depends on how we program the AI and also what the AI is learning.

Let's consider the machine learning aspects of fear.

Suppose you have an AI self-driving car that is learning about driving by observing traffic situations and trying to find patterns to the driving behavior, of which then the AI will adopt those same driving behaviors. In a traffic environment of reasonable human drivers that give proper way to other drivers and abide by legal speeds, the machine learning would find those patterns and presumably be a monkey-see monkey-do and perform driving in the same manner. We have artificial neural networks that indeed do this.

Imagine driving in the chaotic streets of New York City at rush time. Cars cut each other off. Cars drive within inches of other cars. Cars won't let other cars into their lanes. It's a dog eat dog world there. Without knowing the drivers, themselves, and by only looking at the outcomes of their driving, we have a different picture of what driving is all about. Deriving a pattern to driving behavior would be quite a contrast to a traffic environment of a more safety conscious wider-margins-for-error kinds of drivers.

Thus, a neural network or other kind of machine learning will indirectly embody "fear" as it is embodied in the driving behavior of those that the system is learning from. We are not in this case of a machine learning approach explicitly calling out fear and making it part of the AI system as a separate component, and instead it is being captured via the behavior of the driving going on that is being used to pattern after. In one case, the fear of the drivers has led to more collegial driving outcomes, while in the other case the lesser sense of fear leads to cars that nearly hit or actually do include fender benders.

We could though be more explicit about the fear aspects.

The AI self-driving car has sensors that collect data for purposes of sensing the world around the self-driving car, and that data is then fed into the sensor fusion. The sensor fusion tries to figure out from the sensor data what is usable and what might not be, such as having a camera lens that is obscured by dirt and needing to rely instead on a radar that is able to detect that same area that the camera would. The sensor fusion then feeds into a virtual world model that depicts the existing and ongoing state of the surroundings and the self-driving car too.

Based on the virtual world model, the AI needs to derive an action plan of what to do next with the self-driving car. If the situation involves accelerating to get between cars that are to the right of the self-driving car, this is then issued as commands to the controls of the self-driving car. As is the steering command to direct the self-driving car over into the next lane. And so on.

It is within these AI action plans that we are immersing a healthy dose of fear.

You want the self-driving car to be "fearful" of hitting other cars. You want it to be "fearful" of having other drivers hit the self-driving car. These are part of the algorithms of deriving the action plans. If the AI isn't instructed or hasn't learned to not hit other cars, it would likely come up with action plans that inevitably would be intentionally hitting other cars. Indeed, if you have ever watched a simulation that is used to train self-driving cars, you'll see that the self-driving car action plans at first involve hitting other cars, but there is a points mechanism that helps the AI to realize that hitting other cars is not a good thing to do.

By the use of machine learning, we are putting an "instinctive" landscape of fear into the AI of the self-driving car, and this is augmented by an explicitly taught landscape of fear by programmatically developing the AI code accordingly.

Since we are on the topic of fear and AI self-driving cars, I should take a moment to also discuss a whole different aspect about fears and

AI self-driving cars.

There are humans that are fearful of being occupants in AI self-driving cars. I've discussed this at length in various forums and pointed out that though the media at times makes it seem that these are unfounded fears, I assert that people are right to have a healthy dose of fear about riding in today's AI self-driving cars. Notice that I use the word "today's" because I don't want to suggest that we will always be fearful of riding in self-driving cars and instead differentiating that the existing crop of self-driving cars have yet to earn the right to have a low level of fear for occupants.

On a similar vein, some humans are fearful about having AI self-driving cars on our roadways. This is due to a concern that the self-driving cars might hit other cars and strike pedestrians. Once again, I say these people are well justified in such a fear today. AI self-driving cars have yet to provide ample evidence to warrant our being fearless about how these self-driving cars might behave. I don't believe this will be forever and just want to emphasize that it's a condition of the state-of-the-art of what exists today.

Returning back to my mainstay points about including fear into AI self-driving cars, I would want any self-driving car to have a reasonable fear of human drivers. Yes, that's right, be fearful of human drivers. In the same manner that you or I are watching out for other human drivers, and we are leveraging our "fear" to gauge how we drive, it stands to reason that we want the AI self-driving cars to do the same. It needs to be a reasoned fear, and not an unfounded fear. As they say, once the AI has mastered the landscape of fear, the only fear it should have, will be fear itself.

CHAPTER 12
PRE-MORTEM AND
SELF-DRIVING CARS

CHAPTER 12

PRE-MORTEM
AND SELF-DRIVING CARS

I'm sure that you are familiar with the term post-mortem.

We see in the news all the time that when someone dies, and if there are suspicious circumstances, there is a post-mortem done to identify what happened and how the person died. Did the bullet enter into the front or the back of the person? Did they die directly due to the penetration of the bullet, or did they die because they bled out of the bullet hole? Often it takes weeks for a proper post-mortem to be performed. It requires specialized skills, careful examination, and often can produce insights but also create new questions. Suppose there's a knife wound, a bullet wound, and a blow to the head. A post-mortem might be inconclusive about what actually killed the person (any of those three might have done it), or might allow for a multitude of interpretations (one expert says it was the knife, another one says it was the blow to the head).

The concept underlying a post-mortem has gradually found its way into businesses. When a major project falters or fails, there is often a company post-mortem done to figure out what happened. Maybe the company failed to provide sufficient resources to get the project done. Maybe the project had an unrealistic deadline and could not be achieved in the timeline stated. Maybe the project did not gauge what was actually desired to be undertaken and so the final results don't do what was hoped for. And so on.

These post-mortems can be done by internal efforts, while in other cases an outsider is used. If a company thinks that the internal teams cannot be "unbiased" in their introspective assessment, it often is handy to bring in an outsider. There is also value in using an outsider in that they might have special skills at doing post-mortems of business projects. There are methods that can be used and a variety of specialized techniques. Of course, sometimes the internal teams are worried that the outsider is merely being used to undertake a witch hunt. If a project has faltered or failed, there is often a price to pay, and an outsider might be the means to find or allege there is a guilty party, and then off with their heads. To the chagrin of some, at times the true guilty party gets off-the-hook and someone else takes the fall.

In my experience as a seasoned company leader and executive, I always try to focus the post-mortem on trying to find out what we can do to avert such a falter or failing in the future. This does not necessarily mean that a particular person or persons screwed-up per se. It could be that the company processes were the culprit. Or, maybe top management was just as culpable, and though painful to consider, it is something that any good leader needs to be ready to see. Plus, the leadership should not either pre-determine the outcome (sometimes they tell an outsider what outcome they want), and nor should they be reactive during the post-mortem effort.

I actually prefer to refer to the effort as a debriefing or post-project analysis. The use of the word post-mortem has a quite negative connotation. It suggests someone died. In the case of projects, they are rarely of a life and death nature. A leader needs to be aware that some projects will fail, and in fact there are many that advocate that if you aren't failing some of the time that you aren't trying hard enough. When you use the word post-mortem, it conjures up images of death, blood, ugliness, and also for a conventional post-mortem you are looking for the murder weapon and who done it. I'd prefer that the debriefing or post-project analysis of a project be more positive in nature and be about lessons to be learned and changes to be made.

Allow me to introduce another term for a somewhat different aspect, and a term that I'm betting you might not know, pre-mortem.

Yes, the word is pre-mortem. What's that, you might ask?

Pre-Mortem

It is a term used in business to suggest that one way to possibly avoid a project from faltering or failing would be to beforehand try to predict why it might falter or fail. You do this before the project gets underway. This allows you to try and look at the project in a different way.

You normally perceive a project in a start-to-finish manner. You do one step, then the next step, and then the next. As much as possible, you are aiming to make sure that each of the steps do what it they are intended to do. Anticipating potential errors or issues is important. So, you try to build into the project various contingencies, in case things go awry, and you collect metrics in order to try and as early as possible detect when something is amiss.

The sooner you can detect an error or issue, usually the less of an effort and cost to correct it. If you allow an error or issue to fester and permeate the rest of the project, it can become harder to deal with. It's almost like aiming at the moon from the earth, and if your rocket ship veers at the start of the journey, you could end-up millions of miles away from the moon. If your rocket is on-course for most of the distance, and veers toward the tail end, it usually is easier to do a course correction and get back on-track.

For a pre-mortem, you need to think about the project from the finish-to-the-start.

This sometimes sparks you to find potential errors and issues that could otherwise surprisingly arise. Suppose I ask you to read the alphabet in the letter order of A to Z. You have done it a thousand times. You can rattle off each letter without hesitation and without thought. Suppose I then ask you to read the alphabet in order from Z to A. Suddenly, you go much slower. You need to give special attention to the matter. Studies have shown that people reading a list that goes from A to Z, and that had a letter missing or out of sequence, often did not catch the error, due to reading it at lightning speed. Meanwhile, when having to go in the reverse order, they mentally had to calculate each aspect and were more likely to find a letter out of sequence.

That's what can happen when you do a good pre-mortem. It forces you to carefully review each step, and think about what could go wrong. The way you begin is to start by trying to identify ways in which the project outcome could come out wrong. Suppose the project goes over-budget. OK, now, how could that arise? If there are five steps to the project, you'd want to look at which of the steps involves the most expenditure of cost. Aha, the third step will involve the purchase of some needed expensive materials, and if that cost has gone up by the time the third step occurs, it could bust the budget. Having now via the pre-mortem thought of this beforehand, you might decide to go ahead and get the materials now, rather than waiting and getting stuck because the price has gone up when that third step, months from now, gets underway.

Notice that I said the phrase "a good pre-mortem" which is an important distinction in pre-mortems. Just like a post-mortem that gets twisted into becoming a witch hunt, a pre-mortem can get twisted in untoward ways. In some companies, the pre-mortem turns into a political battle, whereby those that want the project are protective and resist any kind of suggested foul outcome, while those that don't want the project to proceed will make-up wildly adverse outcomes. If you can get a wildly adverse outcome to seem plausible and stick, it might scare the stakeholders into deciding to not proceed at all. As such, a pre-mortem carries a danger that it can inadvertently kill a project before it even gets underway.

That being said, there is certainly the chance that the project should not be taking place, and thus the pre-mortem might get everyone to have a more realistic sense of the risks involved. It could be that without a pre-mortem, nobody seriously considered what could go awry. The pre-mortem could save you from a big problem. Generally, though, the notion is that you want the project to succeed, and the pre-mortem helps to further guarantee or at least help assure that it will do so.

In recap, you do a pre-mortem by first trying to identify potentially adverse outcomes, and then you work backward through the steps of the project to try and ascertain how such an outcome could occur. When you find where it could occur, you would then reconfigure the project so that it will either avoid that bad outcome or otherwise try to mitigate its chances of occurring.

In terms of identifying potentially adverse outcomes, some critics of the pre-mortem say that you could spend forever coming up with a zillion bad outcomes.

I am going to invent a new toothbrush. Suppose the toothbrush ends-up harming people's teeth because the bristles are too harsh. This seems like a reasonable kind of bad outcome, meaning that it is something that we all could reasonably agree could go wrong. Suppose someone says that the new toothbrush could have as an outcome that it causes cancer. I dare say that this seems rather farfetched. It's hard to imagine why a toothbrush could cause cancer. Even if you can come up with something oddball to cover it (the toothbrush is made of cancerous materials), it is really a bit out there in terms of a reasonable kind of adverse outcome.

Therefore, I always try to brainstorm for what seem like reasonably reasoned bad outcomes. We might list a comprehensive bunch of bad outcomes, and then review the list for reasonableness. The effort to figure out how each of the outcomes might arise can be substantial, and so you don't want to consume effort unless you think that a particular bad outcome seems plausible. On the other hand, don't knock out of the list bad outcomes that could truly happen, since you are then undermining the point of doing the pre-mortem.

I had one executive that was irked when we suggested that one bad outcome could be that a new system being developed for a major project could create a security hole in their massive database and allow hackers to get into it. He insisted this was "not possible" and that we should strike it from the list. It was such an emotionally charged outcome that he refused to look at the outcome in any impartial manner. Sometimes a pre-mortem needs a delicate hand to get it to occur well.

What does this have to do with AI self-driving cars?

At the Cybernetic Self-Driving Car Institute, we make use of the pre-mortem for our AI development efforts and we urge auto makers and tech firms that are also making AI software for self-driving cars to do the same.

Pre-Mortem Process

Take a look at Figure 1.

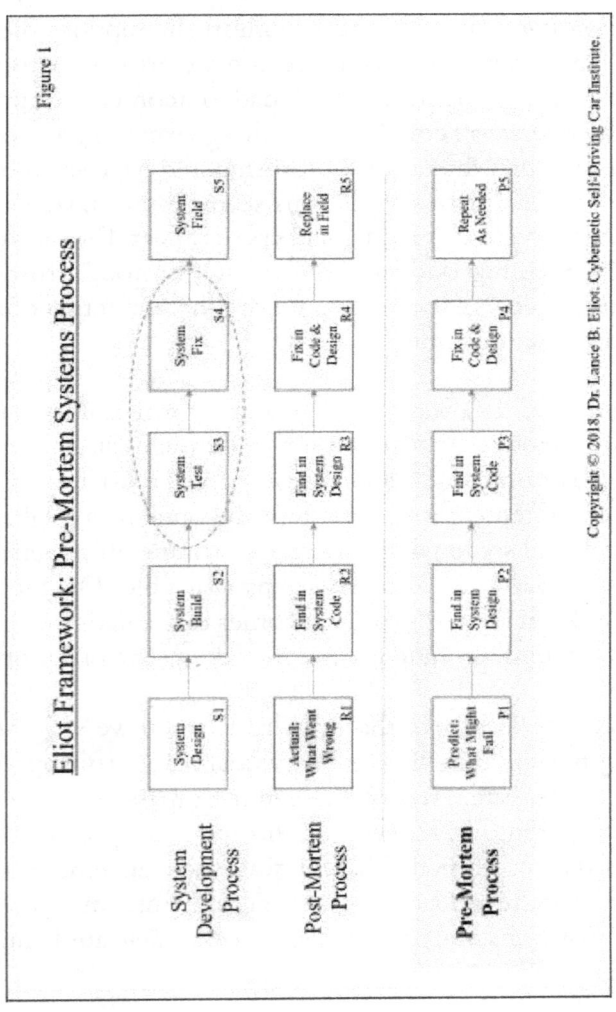

This diagram shows some important systems development processes.

The typical "waterfall" style development effort consists of doing a system design, then a system build, then system testing, then fixes based on the testing, and then fielding of the system. Like most dev shops these days, we are using agile methods and so this portrayal of the classic method is somewhat of a simplification but it gets across the overall points that I want to make.

I've circled the steps that involve the testing and the fixing of the testing bugs or errors discovered. This is the part of the systems development process that involves trying to find errors or issues, and then resolving them.

Suppose we've seeded an error or issue, unknowingly, and we don't find it during the systems development process. In that case, the system gets fielded with a hidden error or issue embedded inside it. Let's hope that the error or issue will not arise at an inopportune time. For your everyday systems like an online dating system, if an error arises it might not be especially life threatening (though maybe it pairs you with the worst date ever).

For AI self-driving cars, since they are life-and-death systems, the testing and the error fixing needs to be extremely rigorous. Some firms are rigorous in this, some are not. Even the ones that are rigorous still have a chance that there's an error or issue that was missed being found and that now exists in the live system that is driving you around in that shiny new self-driving car. You can bet that there's an error or issue hidden somewhere in there. Estimates are that most of the self-driving car software consists of millions of lines of code. I assure you that the code is not going to be perfect. It will have imperfections, for sure.

I am sure that some of you are howling that even if there is an error or issue, it can be readily fixed by an OTA (Over The Air) update to the self-driving car. Yes, that's a possibility. But, meanwhile, I ask you, if the error or issue has to do with say preventing the self-driving car from smacking into a wall, and suppose this actually happens, what then? Sure, if the auto maker or tech firm later finds the error or issue, it can do an update to all such self-driving cars, assuming that the OTA is working properly and that the self-driving cars are doing their OTA updates. Nonetheless, we still have a dead person or people due to the error or issue, and maybe even more deaths until the error or issue is figured out and fixed.

Let's go along with the notion that in fact a self-driving car does smack into a wall. We'd want to do a post-mortem of the AI system and the self-driving car.

In Figure 1, you can see the process for doing a post-mortem of the system.

You start with whatever you know about what actually happened. You then usually will go into the code of the system to try and figure out how it could have led to the adverse outcome. This might also get you to relook at the design of the system. It could be that the error or issue is some isolated bug, or it could be that the system design itself was flawed and so it is a larger matter than seemingly just changing some code.

For the post-mortem of the self-driving car smacking into a wall, we'd want to collect as much information about the nature of the incident as we could get. We'd want to get the black box that presumably resides in the self-driving car. We'd want to know whatever scene analysis has been done in terms of what the conditions were up to and at the crash point, such as whether the streets were wet from rain, and so on. We'd want to examine the memory of the on-board devices. We'd want to see the OTA information of whatever the latest status was of the self-driving car as it communicated with the cloud based updating system. Etc.

Based on whatever we can discover about the incident, the next step in the post-mortem involves searching in the AI system to try and figure out what led to the self-driving car willingly going into the wall. This might involve code inspection. It might involve examining neural networks being used by the AI. And so on.

The question arises as to whether whatever we find could have been possibly found sooner.

As shown in Figure 1, the pre-mortem might have led to discovering whatever the error or issue is, and had we found it during the pre-mortem it might have been corrected prior to the AI self-driving car being fielded.

The pre-mortem process is quite similar to the post-mortem process. You begin with an adverse outcome. In the case of the post-mortem, it's an adverse outcome that actually occurred. In the case of the pre-mortem, it's an adverse outcome that you predict could occur.

For the post-mortem, you usually are first looking into the guts of the system, and then depending upon what you find, you then take a look at the overall design. For a pre-mortem, we typically look at the design first, trying to find a means that the design itself could allow for the adverse outcome. If we find something amiss in the design, then it requires fixing the design and fixing whatever code or system elements are based on the design. Even if we cannot discern any means for the design to produce the adverse outcome, we still need to look at the code and the guts of the system, since it is feasible that the system itself has an error or issue that is otherwise not reflected in the design.

Take a look at Figure 2.

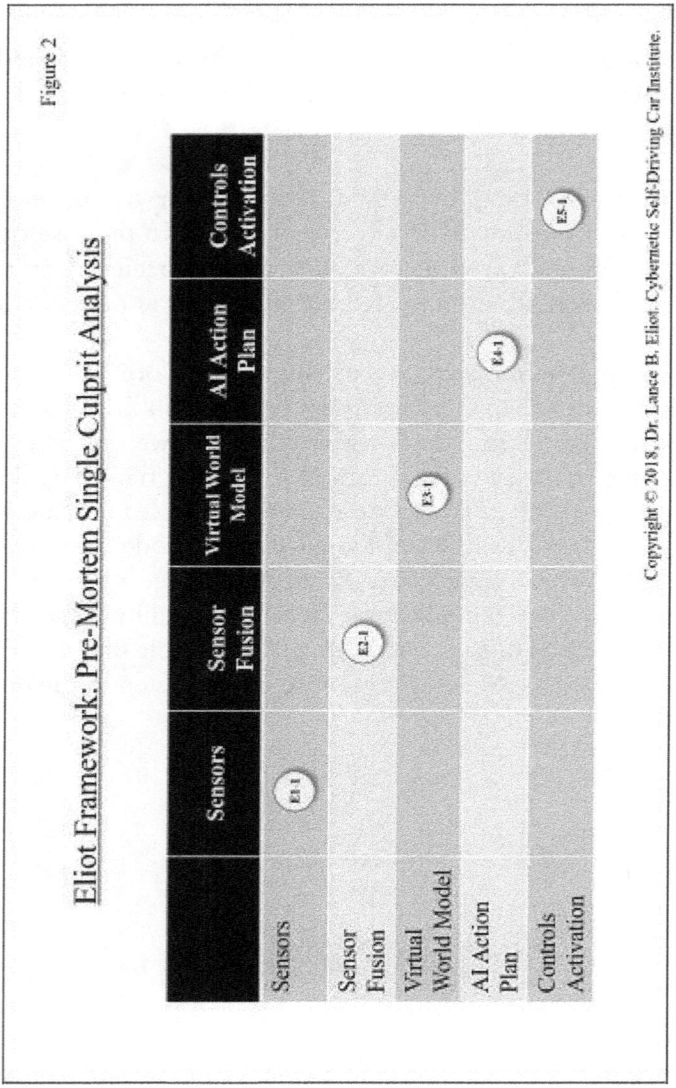

Figure 2

Eliot Framework: Pre-Mortem Single Culprit Analysis

	Sensors	Sensor Fusion	Virtual World Model	AI Action Plan	Controls Activation
Sensors	E1-1				
Sensor Fusion		E2-1			
Virtual World Model			E3-1		
AI Action Plan				E4-1	
Controls Activation					E5-1

Copyright © 2018, Dr. Lance B. Eliot. Cybernetic Self-Driving Car Institute.

When looking for culprits in either the guts of the AI system or in the design, you would usually do so based on the overarching architecture of the AI system that was developed for the self-driving car. This usually consists of at least five major system components, namely the sensors, the sensor fusion, the virtual world model, the AI action plan, and the controls activation.

The sensors provide data about the world surrounding the self-driving car. There is software that collects data from the sensors and tries to interpret the data. This is then fed into the sensor fusion component, which takes the various sensory data and tries to figure out how to best combine it, dealing with some data that is bad, some data that conflicts with other data, and so on. The sensor fusion then leads into updating of the virtual world model. The virtual world model provides a point-in-time indication of the overall status of the self-driving car and its surroundings, as based on the inputs from the sensors and the sensor fusion. The AI then creates an action plan of what the self-driving car should do next, and sends commands via the control activation to the car driving controls. This might include commands to brake, or to speed-up, or to turn, etc.

If we were trying to figure out why the self-driving car ran smack into a wall, the first approach would be to try and find a single culprit. Maybe one of the sensors failed and it led to the catastrophic result (we've labeled as error E1-1). Maybe the sensor fusion had an error and thus misled the rest of the AI (error E2-1). It could be that the virtual world model has an error or issue (E3-1). Or it could be that the AI action plan contained an error or issue (E4-1). Or it could be that the control activation has some kind of error or issue (E5-1).

Sometimes the culprit might indeed be a single culprit. This though is often not the case, and it might be that multiple elements were involved. The nature of the AI of the self-driving car is that it is a quite complex system. There are numerous portions and lots of interconnections. During normal testing, while in system development, many of the single culprit errors or issues are more likely to be found. The tougher ones, the errors or issues involving multiple elements, those are harder to find. Furthermore, some development teams get worn out testing, or use up whatever testing time or resources they had, and so trying to find really obscure errors or issues is often not in the cards.

Rather than focusing on a single culprit, the next level of analyzing would be to look for the double culprit circumstance.

See Figure 3.

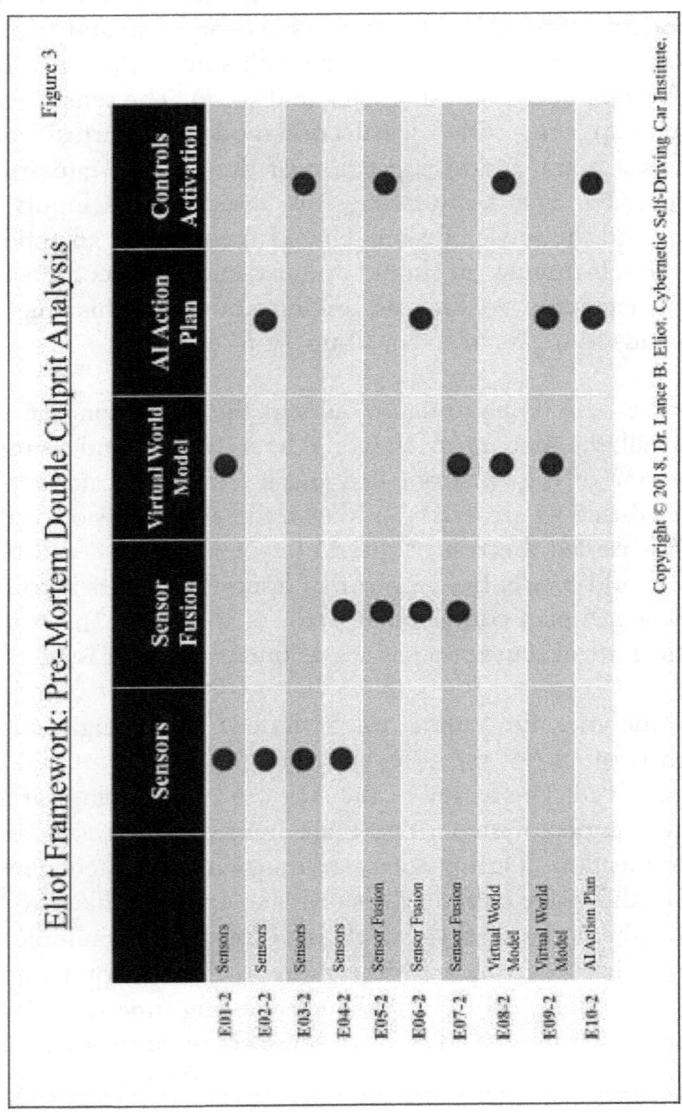

Figure 3

Eliot Framework: Pre-Mortem Double Culprit Analysis

In Figure 3, you can see that there are situations where the error or issue might be found within both the sensors and the sensor fusion (error E01-2). It could be that a sensor reported bad data, the software did not catch it, this was fed into the sensor fusion, the sensor fusion got confused by the bad data, it had no provision of what to do, and thus fed into the virtual world model a false indication that the wall wasn't there. This is a case where two wrongs don't make a right.

You can have a situation where an error in one component happens to cause an error in a second component to arise. In other words, the second error would not have been found, except for the fact that the first component had an error. The two errors might not be directly related to each other. They might have been developed completely separately. That being said, it's also possible that whatever led to the error in the first component, during development, might have also led to an error in the second component. If you have a developer Joe, and he made an error in the first component, and if he is someone that is error prone as a developer, and if he worked also on the second component, you might well have an error in the second component too.

What kind of adverse outcomes should you be considering for an AI self-driving car?

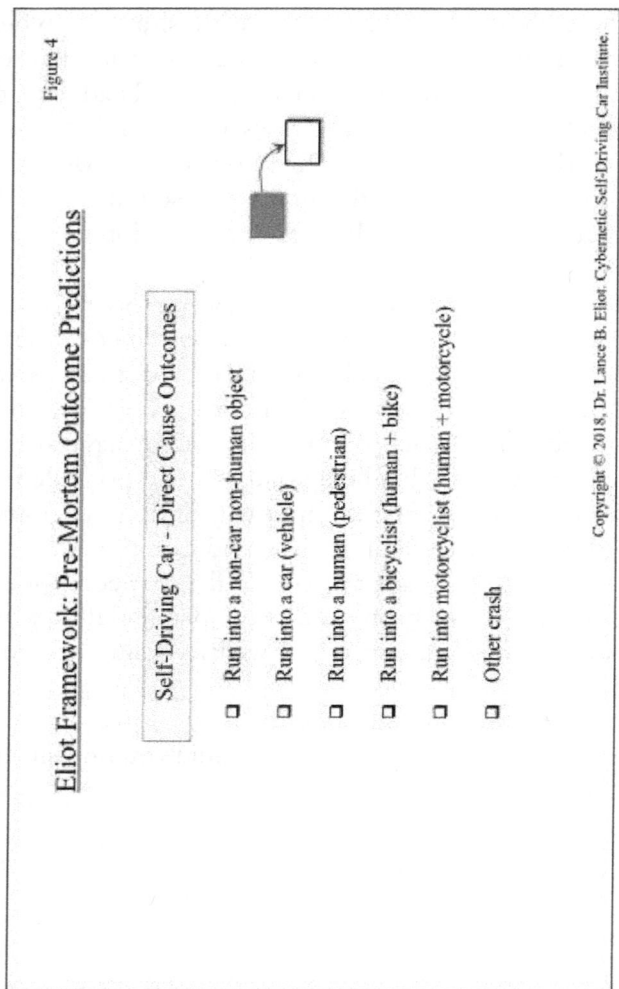

Figure 4

Eliot Framework: Pre-Mortem Outcome Predictions

Self-Driving Car - Direct Cause Outcomes

☐ Run into a non-car non-human object

☐ Run into a car (vehicle)

☐ Run into a human (pedestrian)

☐ Run into a bicyclist (human + bike)

☐ Run into motorcyclist (human + motorcycle)

☐ Other crash

As shown in Figure 4, there are adverse outcomes that are directly caused by the self-driving car. The AI self-driving car might hit a non-car non-human object, such as a tree, a wall, a fire hydrant, and other such objects. You would want to postulate this happening, as a predicted adverse outcome, and try to walk back through the AI and the self-driving car system, in order to try and detect how this could possibly happen.

There are other such adverse outcomes. The self-driving car might hit another car. The other car might be stationary or moving. The self-driving car might be stationary or moving. The self-driving car might hit a pedestrian, or it might hit a bicyclist, or it might hit a motorcyclist. It would be important to also start layering in the conditions that might exist.

For example, we might postulate a scenario whereby the AI self-driving car is driving at night time, on dry roads, and going at a speed of 40 miles per hour, and it runs into a pedestrian. These are more specific conditions and it will make it more amenable to then trying to discern how the AI system could allow this to occur.

The pre-mortem can also involve examining adverse outcomes that aren't necessarily a directly caused incident by the AI self-driving car.

See Figure 5.

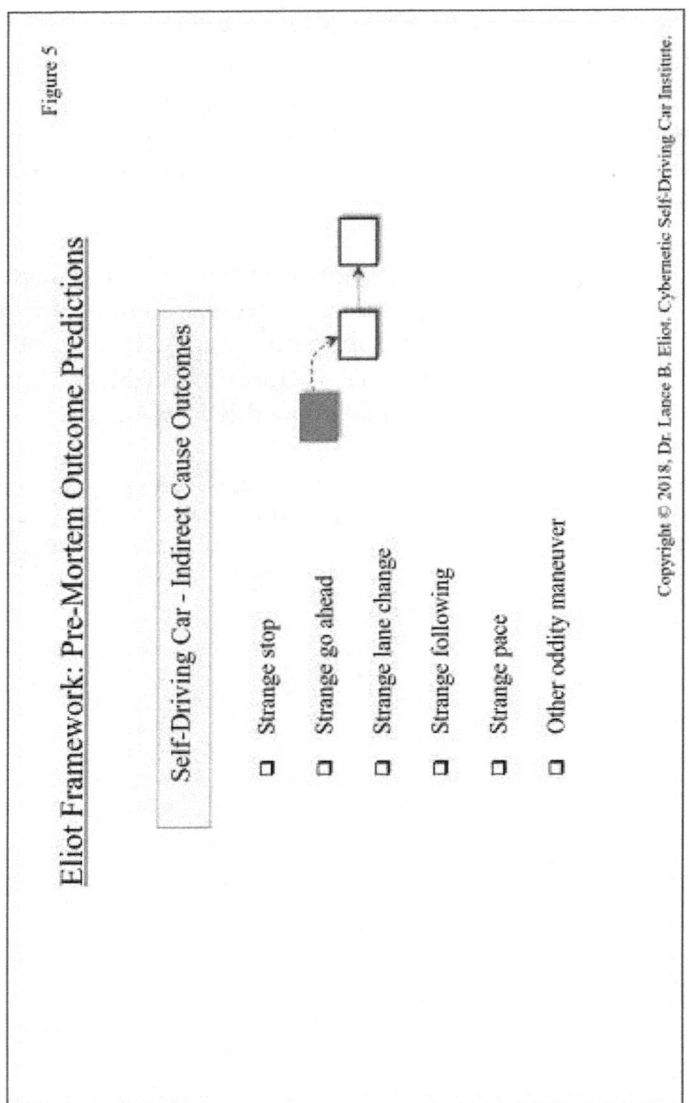

Figure 5

Eliot Framework: Pre-Mortem Outcome Predictions

Self-Driving Car - Indirect Cause Outcomes

☐ Strange stop

☐ Strange go ahead

☐ Strange lane change

☐ Strange following

☐ Strange pace

☐ Other oddity maneuver

Various indirect causes include that the AI self-driving car just suddenly seems to come to a stop, or suddenly seems to rush ahead, or suddenly seems to change lanes. Even though the self-driving car perhaps won't hit and harm anyone due to these actions, it might cause another car to react and turn into a car crash. If the AI self-driving car suddenly switches lanes, and cuts off a car coming in that lane, the other car might swerve to avoid hitting the AI self-driving car, and then the swerving car loses control and rams into a telephone pole. The AI self-driving car was "innocent" of being in the accident, but was a factor in producing the accident. These are worthy of a pre-mortem assessment too.

Few of the auto makers and tech firms that are making AI self-driving car systems are doing pre-mortems. It's an approach not widely used overall. But, for the case of systems that involve life-and-death kinds of systems, doing a pre-mortem adds more confidence to being able to field a system that has less chances of having disastrous errors or issues.

Some AI developers say to me that you can never fully find all errors or issues beforehand, and thus they seem to imply that there's no point in doing things like a pre-mortem. I don't buy into that logic. It's the proverbial throwing the baby out with the bath water. We need to try and do as much testing of AI self-driving cars as we can. Shrugging your shoulders and waving your hands is not a valid method of testing. The pre-mortem is not a guarantee of eliminating hidden errors or issues, but it is handy tool to ferret out as many as we can. Better safe than sorry.

CHAPTER 13

KITS

AND SELF-DRIVING CARS

CHAPTER 13
KITS
AND SELF-DRIVING CARS

Suppose that you invented an innovative device for automobiles that every car owner wanted to eagerly buy so they can put it onto or into their car. Let's call the invention the thingamabob. Congrats on inventing something that everyone wants.

You decide to price the thingamabob at one dollar. There are about 270 million cars in the United States alone, and so after you've sold your thingamabob to every U.S. car owner, you have a revenue of around $270 million dollars. That's impressive.

Turns out that instead of pricing it at one dollar, you opt to price it at $100 per thingamabob. In that case, your revenue is a whopping $27,000,000,000 (that's 27 billion dollars!). But, wait, you realize that your invention is worth its weight in gold, so you price it at $1,000, and now your revenue is $27 trillion dollars. After further thought, you decide that it should really be priced at $100,000, and now your revenue is in the stratosphere of trillions and in the quadrillions and upwards.

That's a lot of money.

And in fact, this is illustrative of why there is a feverish desire to develop a car kit that would turn everyday automobiles into AI self-driving cars. Imagine that if you could put together a car kit that would allow conventional cars to be converted into becoming AI self-driving cars, you'd be sought by all. Auto makers would rush to your door.

221

Tech firms would be at your feet. You'd be beloved by all those that are craving to get to AI self-driving cars for the masses. Probably a Nobel prize would be in your future.

If you hear or see something that says the XYZ Company is developing a kit for AI self-driving cars, on the one hand it is bound to perk your interest, but on the other hand I'd suggest you take a critical eye to whatever you are told or hear in this regard. The rush toward this particular pot of gold is filled with many misleading claims, and some outright false claims, and a hefty dose of pure scams.

So, before you plunk down big bucks as an angel investor or private equity or venture capitalist, make sure to read the fine print about whatever kind of AI self-driving car kit that someone is trying to say they are inventing. I'll be generous for the moment and say that the existing claims of those working on kits is that they are generally sincere in their pursuits, though at times it can be a bit hazy about what they are truly working on.

At the Cybernetic Self-Driving Car Institute, we are advising firms that are desirous of developing AI self-driving car kits (and, we are also making some of the elements for AI self-driving car kits).

Allow me a moment to explain what AI self-driving car kits are all about.

Defining Self-Driving Car Kits

I describe the AI self-driving car kits marketspace as consisting of three fundamental approaches. Take a look at Figure 1 and look at the tree structure that's on the left side of the diagram.

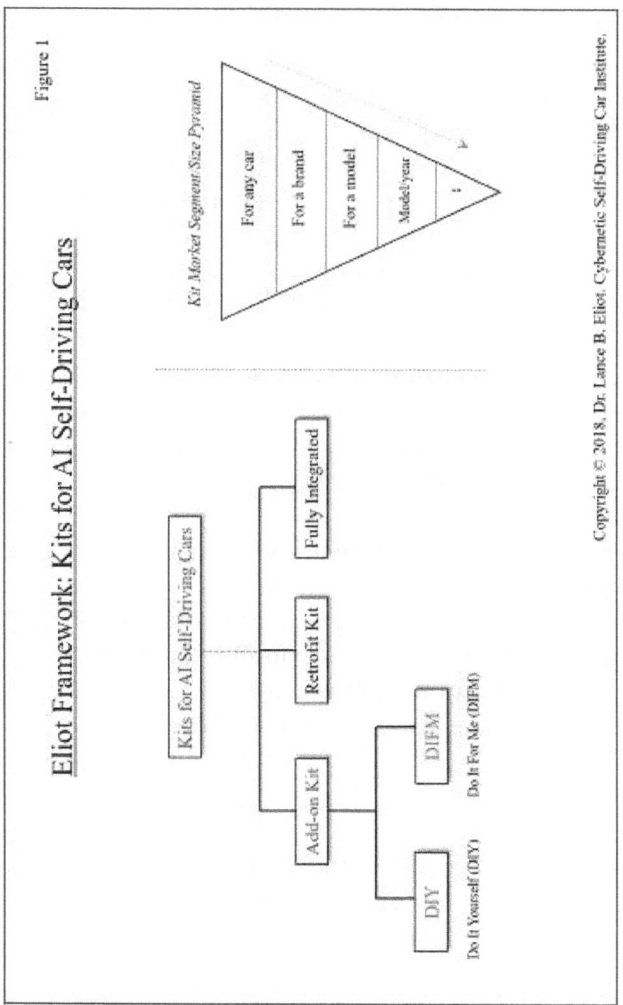

Figure 1

Eliot Framework: Kits for AI Self-Driving Cars

Copyright © 2018, Dr. Lance B. Eliot, Cybernetic Self-Driving Car Institute.

There is the Add-on Kit approach, which consists of add-on elements that are not already native to the car itself and involves installing the kit elements onto and into the car. This add-on kit is typically provided by a third-party and not the actual auto maker. An auto maker could certainly opt to make and sell the add-on kits, and I am not ruling out the possibility, so I am just suggesting that right now these AI self-driving car kits are being crafted by third-parties, typically a tech company. I'd predict that anyone actually successful in providing an AI self-driving car kit is a candidate to be bought up by the auto maker or bought up by some other larger tech firm or other firms interested in the auto industry. It's a sweet spot, for sure.

For the add-on kit, the question arises as to who is going to actually install the kit onto your car. This divides into the do-it-yourself (DIY) kit versus the do-it-for-me (DIFM) kit. For AI self-driving cars, the odds of making a kit that is DIY is pretty low right now. I say this because by-and-large a kit to genuinely do any real AI self-driving car aspects is going to be complex to install and setup. Having your average consumer be able to do this is unlikely. Even having a car hobbyist do this is unlikely. The more likely scenario currently is that it would be kit that involves DIFM. You would need to take your car to some expert installers that are versed in the kit and the nature of the car that the kit is aimed to work on.

When I earlier mentioned the thingamabob, I discussed the pricing aspects of $1, $100, $1,000, and $100,000. If a kit costs $1,000, and the installation effort costs an additional $10,000, the notion of considering the kit cost alone is admittedly understated. You need to also consider the cost for installing and setting up the kit. In this simple example of a $1K kit and $10K install, the effort to do the install and setup dwarfs the actual product cost. We'll come back to the topic of costs later on.

The second approach is the Retrofit. This is typically something done by the auto maker and involves taking an existing car line and retrofitting it with the AI self-driving car kit. The auto maker or its authorized installation partners would do this retrofitting. One advantage is that the retrofit is likely to be more emmeshed into the car, versus the add-on kit, and tends to be less obtrusive and seemingly as though it really was almost a part of the car when the car was first developed.

The third approach is the Fully Integrated kit. In one sense, this is not necessarily even a kit in the traditional sense. The car when designed has been developed with the AI self-driving car capabilities from the ground-up. Those elements that are there for the AI self-driving car purposes are technically considered part of the "kit" that made the car into an AI self-driving car.

AI Self-Driving Car Kit Markets

For those of you interested in AI self-driving car kits, you might consider the nature of the market for those kits. As further shown in Figure 1, there's a pyramid that depicts the market aspects.

If you could make an AI self-driving car kit that could fit onto and into any kind of conventional car, regardless of brand or model, you'd have hit the bonanza. This would suggest that you'd be able to possibly sell this kit to any of the 270 million car owners in the United States alone. Thus, I show the "any car" is at the top of the pyramid as it has the largest market potential.

Below the "any car" is the specific brand segment. In this case, the AI self-driving car kit only works for a particular auto maker's cars and for one or more of their specific brands. Beneath that segment would be the narrower arena of just a specific model of a car that's within a specific brand that's within a particular auto maker. We could also toss into this the year of the car, since it is likely going to be harder to have a kit that applies equally to older versions of a particular car. And so on.

Now, don't be discouraged if you are aiming at an AI self-driving car kit that's for a particular type of car. Though it means that your market size is smaller than if you aimed larger, you still have a potential of a sizable market. Think about all of those American muscle cars like the Ford Mustang that are in circulation and still being sold. It would still be a hefty sized market if you decided that was your target for your AI self-driving car kit. Plus, presumably, once successful there, you could hopefully reuse some of your kit toward making the same kind of thing for other lines of cars.

Scope of an AI Self-Driving Car Kit

One of the major confusions about AI self-driving car kits is the aspect of what they actually do. For someone to say that they are making an AI self-driving car kit, it sounds like a really ambitious effort and implies that they will magically turn a car into a fully true AI self-driving car. Not so fast!

Take a look at Figure 2.

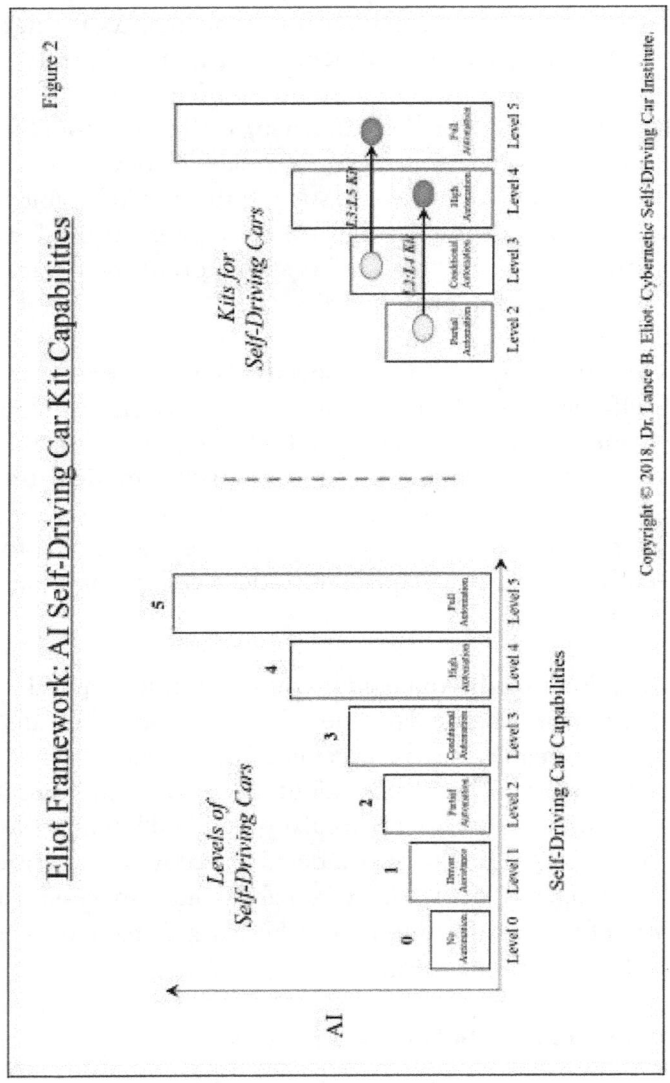

On the left side of the figure, I show the levels of self-driving cars.

This is the standard promulgated by the Society for Automotive Engineers (SAE) and has become well accepted in the self-driving car industry. There is the lowest or least level of automation that is referred to as Level 0, essentially no automation, and ranges up the highest or most level of automation, referred to as the vaunted and desirable Level 5. Pretty much, anyone that is serious about self-driving cars is seeking to reach Level 5.

It's great to get to the other levels, such as the Level 3 and Level 4, and there is lots of money to be made by automation at those levels, but the big fish, the kind of kings, that's the Level 5 (a self-driving car that involves AI that can drive a car as though a human could and requires no human intervention in the driving task). I don't want to discourage anyone from aiming at the Level 3 and Level 4. Some say that we need to get there first, before we can get to Level 5. Others say that Level 3 and Level 4 are a distraction and thus forget about those and aim at the Level 5. We'll see how this plays out.

The reason it's crucial to understand that there are levels of self-driving car is so that you can ferret out the claims of someone that says they are making an AI self-driving car kit. What does their kit do? Does it make a self-driving car that is at Level 5? Or at Level 4? Or at Level 3? Or what? You cannot assume that when someone says they have a kit for turning a car into a self-driving car that it means it is turning the car into a Level 5.

Unfortunately, the mass media usually grabs ahold of announcements by an AI self-driving car kit maker and generates bold headlines that the AI self-driving car kit is nearly here. When you dig into it, you'll likely discover it's not at all a Level 5 oriented kit. Some of you might remember the tremendous buzz when George Hotz was pursuing his self-driving car kit in 2016 and also saying that it would cost just $1,000. This produced huge headlines. How exciting that the classic "put together in a garage by a bunch of nerds" type of story was going to leap us all forward into the Level 5 self-driving car world. It was touted by the media as a kit that would be as easy to install as assembling Ikea furniture. As those of us in the self-driving car industry knew, it wasn't aimed at Level 5 and there were other aspects about its scope that the major media gave scant attention to. The story did though provide inspiration for many that hadn't thought it possible to even consider making a kit, and so in that sense the headlines spurred others accordingly.

In Figure 2, on the right side of the diagram, I show that the AI self-driving car kits tend to make a base assumption about the existing level of the car, and then by installing and using the kit that you can turn that car into a higher level. Let's use a notation of stating that the assumed base level of the car as a L0, L1, L2, L3, L4, or L5, and the target is also one of those designations, and we'll use a left-to-right reading protocol of stating the base first, followed by a colon, ending with the target level.

As an example, consider this: L2:L4. This means that a particular AI self-driving car kit assumes that the existing car is at a Level 2, and that by installing and using the kit that the car will act like a Level 4. Another example would be L3:L5. That's a kit that assumes a Level 3 car and then upon installing and using the kit we'd have a Level 5 car.

This is a handy nomenclature. Whenever anyone starts claiming they are making an AI self-driving car kit, you should ask them what is the assumed base level and what is the targeted level. These are radically different in that taking a Level 2 car to a Level 5 (L2:L5) is going to be generally a much harder feat, in comparison to say taking a Level 4 to a Level 5

(L4:L5). One of the main reasons why the feat is much harder for L2:L5 than a L4:L5 is that the higher the level the car already is, the more that the kit can leverage about what is already there. If the kit has to take on more of the core aspects of a self-driving car, it is going to be usually be much more complex and elaborate. Easier to just build on top of what is already there, and thus the further along the car is to start with, the better it can be for the kit.

Mixture of Car & Kit

Part of the reason that an AI self-driving car kit is going to be more particular and less of a universal type of kit involves the aspect that the kit needs to integrate with the car. The specifics of the car controls on a car made by one auto maker are going to be different than the car controls of another car maker. The nature of the electronics systems is going to be different. And so on. It's a mess in that there's not really just one standard way that all cars are designed and made.

Imagine if you were making an add-on for a smartphone. You might create the add-on for the Apple iPhone. But, it's unlikely it would then work for an Android phone. Trying to make something universal for things that aren't universal in their design and approach is a tough act. For now, expect that most of the AI self-driving car kits are going to be targeted at a specific make of car. That's reality.

Take a look at Figure 3.

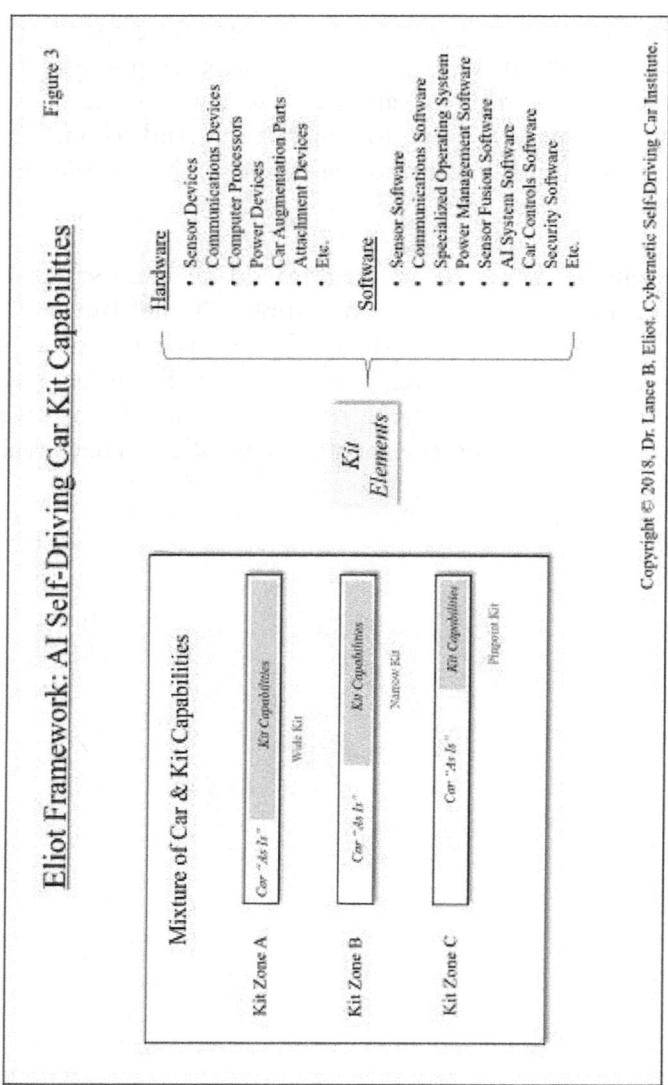

Figure 3

Eliot Framework: AI Self-Driving Car Kit Capabilities

Copyright © 2018, Dr. Lance B. Eliot, Cybernetic Self-Driving Car Institute.

We define three zones of the mixing of the car and the kit capabilities. There's Kit Zone A, which consists of a "wide kit" that has to do a lot and the car itself is not bringing much to the table for doing the AI self-driving car aspects. There's the Kit Zone B consisting of a narrower kit due to the aspect that the car already has some amount of AI self-driving car capabilities and the kit leverages those. Then there's the Kit Zone C that involves a car that has a lot of AI self-driving car capabilities and so the kit can do less. All of this is a relative notion, meaning that without respect to the levels of the car, this is just saying that there are more or less elements needed in the kit as dependent upon what the car provides.

The types of AI self-driving car kit elements can be divided into hardware and software, as shown on the right side of Figure 3.

The hardware typically involves this:

- Sensor Devices
- Communications Devices
- Computer Processors
- Power Devices
- Car Augmentation Parts
- Attachment Devices
- Etc.

The software typically involves this:

- Sensor Software
- Communications Software
- Specialized Operating System
- Power Management Software
- Sensor Fusion Software
- AI System Software
- Car Controls Software
- Security Software
- Etc.

There might be additional hardware and additional software elements beyond what I've listed. There is also the chance that there might be less elements involved. A kit might be only taking on a smaller piece of the automation and so it is aimed at just say the sensors.

This brings up the other notion that there are the all-in-one kits and there are the subcomponent kits. You might have someone that makes a kit to put LIDAR onto your AI self-driving car. Someone else makes a kit to do the car controls. These various kits might be made and sold individually. There is also the possibility that someone combines those together into one all-in-one kit.

Keep in mind too that some of the kit elements might be intended as being a supplement to what is already on the car, while other kit elements are intended to replace the original equipment parts. You might for example put a supplemental element that attaches to the accelerator pedal and will push down on it to cause acceleration, and other such supplemental element that attaches to the brakes and one that attaches to the steering wheel. Or, it could be that someone makes a replacement accelerator pedal, a replacement brake pedal, and a replacement steering wheel, which then replaces those already in the car and you make use of these new elements instead.

Important Safety and Liability Concerns

There is already a huge conventional automotive aftermarket aimed at augmenting cars and also aimed at simply replacing the wear-and-tear parts of conventional cars. There has been an increasing rise in the distance driven per conventional car and the average age of cars is around 11.6 years in the United States, trending toward people hanging onto their cars longer. Cars being kept longer and being driven more is a good thing for the car aftermarket. Some statistics say that we spent $300 billion per year just a few years ago and that by the year 2024 it will jump to $680 billion.

Just imagine how high the auto aftermarket could go if we start to see viable AI self-driving car kits being sold.

Speaking of which, I promised earlier that I would poke further into the costs of buying an AI self-driving car kit.

Realistically, a kit for $1,000 is going to be a marginal kit, meaning that it will not do much in terms of making a car into a true AI self-driving car. Some of these low-end kits are aimed at making a conventional car become a Level 2, so it purports to do this: L1:L2. Well, you might not be very happy with this kind of AI self-driving car, especially when you look closely and realize that there are a ton of limitations as to what the kit provides – for example, the kit assumes that there are lane markings on the road, and so the moment that you are driving along and the road markings aren't there, you as the human driver need to right away take over the controls.

The odds are that a true AI self-driving car kit is going to more akin to costing in the tens of thousands of dollars. Let's pretend for the moment that a kit comes to the market at a cost of $100,000 to purchase it (ignoring the installation costs for the moment). You might say that few people could afford the $100,000 and so this is not going to sell very well. That's partially true. Keep in mind that presumably a true AI self-driving car could become a ridesharing vehicle that generates revenue for you. You might use your now transformed self-driving car to take you to work, and then the rest of the day it is being used by others that are paying to use your self-driving car. It might therefore make financial sense to go ahead and buy that $100,000 kit, doing so via some kind of loan or other financial approach, knowing that it will ultimately "pay for itself" possibly.

What we haven't yet covered in all of this discussion about AI self-driving car kits is the bigger questions about safety and liability.

Would you be willing to trust that your car when using a $1,000 self-driving car kit is going to properly work on our roadways and you'll be perfectly safe in using it?

Right now, people are reluctant to get into a self-driving car that has a gigantic auto maker or tech firm backing it, which they've invested millions upon millions in developing, and so imagine that you are going to use a self-driving car that was augmented by a kit from an unknown start-up. I am not saying that you should be saying no, and only bringing up that we would want to know that somehow this thingamabob has been sufficiently tested for safety purposes.

Where does an AI self-driving car kit fit into the federal regulations about cars, and the state and local regulations about cars? Who would certify that the use of the kit will produce a safe self-driving car? What does safe mean in this context? There is a myriad of such questions.

The zillion dollar question involves liability.

If the kit is put onto your car, and your now transformed self-driving car gets into an accident, who has the liability for the accident if the kit played a part in the cause of the accident? You could argue too that the kit might only be 1% of the cause of the accident, or maybe it's 100%, but either way the kit is going to certainly be considered a factor in whatever accident happens.

Are you as the owner solely responsible for whatever the kit did? The odds are that everyone else in the food chain is going to get some liability attached. The maker of the kit. The installer of the kit. A mechanic that maybe worked on your car and somehow touched the kit. A previous owner that maybe put the kit into the car and you now are claiming that you didn't know that the kit would do this or that. The list of culpable parties is pretty long. An astute lawyer is bound to go after any of those in the food chain, regardless of whether there is substantive proof per se that the kit was a factor or not.

In short, the path to viable AI self-driving car kits is going to be a gauntlet that involves navigating the safety issues and the liability issues. I suppose you could say that with the prospects of big bucks comes the dangers of big risks.

Will we soon see AI self-driving car kits for sell on Amazon and eBay Motors (those are considered the two largest sellers of aftermarket auto parts and accessories in the United States)? Well, if you do, make sure to consider what the kit actually does, look at the fine print, and consider the safety and liability aspects.

If we could wave a magic wand and have AI self-driving car kits, it would be a tremendous boon towards getting us toward a world of AI self-driving cars. There is pent up demand for this. The auto makers and tech firms realize this too. Many of them are making investments in firms that are doing some kind of kits, whether an all-in-one or piecemeal, whether an add-on versus retrofit, etc. These firms all realize that there is a pot of gold to be found. Let's get to the pot of gold with a mindset of ensuring that the sought riches come with a need to be safe and sound.

APPENDIX

Lance B. Eliot

APPENDIX A

TEACHING WITH THIS MATERIAL

The material in this book can be readily used either as a supplemental to other content for a class, or it can also be used as a core set of textbook material for a specialized class. Classes where this material is most likely used include any classes at the college or university level that want to augment the class by offering thought provoking and educational essays about AI and self-driving cars.

In particular, here are some aspects for class use:

o   <u>Computer Science</u>. Studying AI, autonomous vehicles, etc.

o   <u>Business</u>. Exploring technology and it adoption for business.

o   <u>Sociology</u>. Sociological views on the adoption and advancement of technology.

Specialized classes at the undergraduate and graduate level can also make use of this material.

For each chapter, consider whether you think the chapter provides material relevant to your course topic. There is plenty of opportunity to get the students thinking about the topic and force them to decide whether they agree or disagree with the points offered and positions taken. I would also encourage you to have the students do additional research beyond the chapter material presented (I provide next some suggested assignments they can do).

RESEARCH ASSIGNMENTS ON THESE TOPICS

Your students can find background material on these topics, doing so in various business and technical publications. I list below the top ranked AI related journals. For business publications, I would suggest the usual culprits such as the Harvard Business Review, Forbes, Fortune, WSJ, and the like.

Here are some suggestions of homework or projects that you could assign to students:

a) <u>Assignment for foundational AI research topic</u>: Research and prepare a paper and a presentation on a specific aspect of Deep AI, Machine Learning, ANN, etc. The paper should cite at least 3 reputable sources. Compare and contrast to what has been stated in this book.

b) <u>Assignment for the Self-Driving Car topic</u>: Research and prepare a paper and Self-Driving Cars. Cite at least 3 reputable sources and analyze the characterizations. Compare and contrast to what has been stated in this book.

c) <u>Assignment for a Business topic</u>: Research and prepare a paper and a presentation on businesses and advanced technology. What is hot, and what is not? Cite at least 3 reputable sources. Compare and contrast to the depictions in this book.

d) <u>Assignment to do a Startup:</u> Have the students prepare a paper about how they might startup a business in this realm. They must submit a sound Business Plan for the startup. They could also be asked to present their Business Plan and so should also have a presentation deck to coincide with it.

You can certainly adjust the aforementioned assignments to fit to your particular needs and the class structure. You'll notice that I ask for 3 reputable cited sources for the paper writing based assignments. I usually steer students toward "reputable" publications, since otherwise they will cite some oddball source that has no credentials other than that they happened to write something and post it onto the Internet. You can define "reputable" in whatever way you prefer, for example some faculty think Wikipedia is not reputable while others believe it is reputable and allow students to cite it.

The reason that I usually ask for at least 3 citations is that if the student only does one or two citations they usually settle on whatever they happened to find the fastest. By requiring three citations, it usually seems to force them to look around, explore, and end-up probably finding five or more, and then whittling it down to 3 that they will actually use.

I have not specified the length of their papers, and leave that to you to tell the students what you prefer. For each of those assignments, you could end-up with a short one to two pager, or you could do a dissertation length paper. Base the length on whatever best fits for your class, and the credit amount of the assignment within the context of the other grading metrics you'll be using for the class.

I mention in the assignments that they are to do a paper and prepare a presentation. I usually try to get students to present their work. This is a good practice for what they will do in the business world. Most of the time, they will be required to prepare an analysis and present it. If you don't have the class time or inclination to have the students present, then you can of course cut out the aspect of them putting together a presentation.

If you want to point students toward highly ranked journals in AI, here's a list of the top journals as reported by *various citation counts sources* (this list changes year to year):

o   Communications of the ACM

o   Artificial Intelligence

o   Cognitive Science

o   IEEE Transactions on Pattern Analysis and Machine Intelligence

o   Foundations and Trends in Machine Learning

o   Journal of Memory and Language

o   Cognitive Psychology

o   Neural Networks

o   IEEE Transactions on Neural Networks and Learning Systems

o   IEEE Intelligent Systems

o   Knowledge-based Systems

GUIDE TO USING THE CHAPTERS

For each of the chapters, I provide next some various ways to use the chapter material. You can assign the tasks as individual homework assignments, or the tasks can be used with team projects for the class. You can easily layout a series of assignments, such as indicating that the students are to do item "a" below for say Chapter 1, then "b" for the next chapter of the book, and so on.

a) What is the main point of the chapter and describe in your own words the significance of the topic,

b) Identify at least two aspects in the chapter that you agree with, and support your concurrence by providing at least one other outside researched item as support; make sure to explain your basis for disagreeing with the aspects,

c) Identify at least two aspects in the chapter that you disagree with, and support your disagreement by providing at least one other outside researched item as support; make sure to explain your basis for disagreeing with the aspects,

d) Find an aspect that was not covered in the chapter, doing so by conducting outside research, and then explain how that aspect ties into the chapter and what significance it brings to the topic,

e) Interview a specialist in industry about the topic of the chapter, collect from them their thoughts and opinions, and readdress the chapter by citing your source and how they compared and contrasted to the material,

f) Interview a relevant academic professor or researcher in a college or university about the topic of the chapter, collect from them their thoughts and opinions, and readdress the chapter by citing your source and how they compared and contrasted to the material,

g) Try to update a chapter by finding out the latest on the topic, and ascertain whether the issue or topic has now been solved or whether it is still being addressed, explain what you come up with.

The above are all ways in which you can get the students of your class involved in considering the material of a given chapter. You could mix things up by having one of those above assignments per each week, covering the chapters over the course of the semester or quarter.

As a reminder, here are the chapters of the book and you can select whichever chapters you find most valued for your particular class:

Companion Book By This Author

Advances in AI and Autonomous Vehicles: Cybernetic Self-Driving Cars

Practical Advances in Artificial Intelligence (AI) and Machine Learning
by
Dr. Lance B. Eliot, MBA, PhD

This title is available via Amazon and other book sellers

Companion Book By This Author

Self-Driving Cars:
"The Mother of All AI Projects"

by Dr. Lance B. Eliot, MBA, PhD

This title is available via Amazon and other book sellers

Companion Book By This Author

Innovation and Thought Leadership on Self-Driving Driverless Cars

by Dr. Lance B. Eliot, MBA, PhD

Chapter Title

This title is available via Amazon and other book sellers

Companion Book By This Author

New Advances in AI Autonomous Driverless Cars Self-Driving Cars

by Dr. Lance B. Eliot, MBA, PhD

Chapter Title

This title is available via Amazon and other book sellers

Companion Book By This Author

Introduction to
Driverless Self-Driving Cars

by Dr. Lance B. Eliot, MBA, PhD

Chapter Title

This title is available via Amazon and other book sellers

Companion Book By This Author
Autonomous Vehicle Driverless Self-Driving Cars and Artificial Intelligence
by Dr. Lance B. Eliot, MBA, PhD

Chapter Title

This title is available via Amazon and other book sellers

Companion Book By This Author

Transformative Artificial Intelligence
Driverless Self-Driving Cars

by Dr. Lance B. Eliot, MBA, PhD

This title is available via Amazon and other book sellers

ABOUT THE AUTHOR

Dr. Lance B. Eliot, MBA, PhD is the CEO of Techbruim, Inc. and Executive Director of the Cybernetic Self-Driving Car Institute, and has over twenty years of industry experience including serving as a corporate officer in a billion dollar firm and was a partner in a major executive services firm. He is also a serial entrepreneur having founded, ran, and sold several high-tech related businesses. He previously hosted the popular radio show *Technotrends* that was also available on American Airlines flights via their in-flight audio program. Author or co-author of a dozen books and over 400 articles, he has made appearances on CNN, and has been a frequent speaker at industry conferences.

A former professor at the University of Southern California (USC), he founded and led an innovative research lab on Artificial Intelligence in Business. Known as the "AI Insider" his writings on AI advances and trends has been widely read and cited. He also previously served on the faculty of the University of California Los Angeles (UCLA), and was a visiting professor at other major universities. He was elected to the International Board of the Society for Information Management (SIM), a prestigious association of over 3,000 high-tech executives worldwide.

He has performed extensive community service, including serving as Senior Science Adviser to the Vice Chair of the Congressional Committee on Science & Technology. He has served on the Board of the OC Science & Engineering Fair (OCSEF), where he is also has been a Grand Sweepstakes judge, and likewise served as a judge for the Intel International SEF (ISEF). He served as the Vice Chair of the Association for Computing Machinery (ACM) Chapter, a prestigious association of computer scientists. Dr. Eliot has been a shark tank judge for the USC Mark Stevens Center for Innovation on start-up pitch competitions, and served as a mentor for several incubators and accelerators in Silicon Valley and Silicon Beach. He served on several Boards and Committees at USC, including having served on the Marshall Alumni Association (MAA) Board in Southern California.

Dr. Eliot holds a PhD from USC, MBA, and Bachelor's in Computer Science, and earned the CDP, CCP, CSP, CDE, and CISA certifications. Born and raised in Southern California, and having traveled and lived internationally, he enjoys scuba diving, surfing, and sailing.

ADDENDUM

Disruptive Artificial Intelligence (AI) And Driverless Self-Driving Cars

Practical Advances in Artificial Intelligence and Machine Learning

By

Dr. Lance B. Eliot, MBA, PhD

———

For supplemental materials of this book, visit:

www.ai-selfdriving-cars.guru

For special orders of this book, contact:

LBE Press Publishing

Email: LBE.Press.Publishing@gmail.com